THE SPIRIT OF PSYCHOTHERAPY

THE SPIRIT
OF PSYCHOTHERAPY
A Hidden Dimension

Jeremy Holmes

KARNAC
firing the mind

First published in 2024 by
Karnac Books Limited
62 Bucknell Road
Bicester
Oxfordshire OX26 2DS

British Library Cataloguing in Publication Data

A C.I.P. for this book is available from the British Library

ISBN: 978-1-91349-480-3 (paperback)
ISBN: 978-1-91349-481-0 (e-book)

Typeset by Medlar Publishing Solutions Pvt Ltd, India

www.firingthemind.com

In memory of Ros Holmes

16/02/1943–07/10/2021

The Sea of Faith
Was once, too, at the full, and round earth's shore
Lay like the folds of a bright girdle furled.
But now I only hear
Its melancholy, long, withdrawing roar,
Retreating …
Ah love, let us be true
To one another! …

—Mathew Arnold, *Dover Beach*

O man-projected Figure, of late
Imaged as we, thy knell who shall survive?
Whence came it we were tempted to create
One whom we can no longer keep alive?

—Thomas Hardy, *God's Funeral*

If we had a keen vision and feeling of all ordinary human life,
it would be like hearing the grass grow and the squirrel's heart
beat, and we should die of that roar which lies on the other side
of silence.

—George Eliot, *Middlemarch*

Contents

Acknowledgements

As always, this book could not have been written without the support and helpful comments and criticisms of family, friends, colleagues, and patients, as well as the background infrastructure of the Department of Psychoanalytic Studies in the University of Exeter. I hope all will accept my gratitude and excuse its many mistakes and failings. I am especially indebted to Jon Allen, Eva Townsend Bilton, John Duncan, Andrew Elder, Ben Griffin, Jacob Holmes, Graham Music, Charles Montgomery, and Kristin White, who somehow found the time in their busy lives to read and make extremely helpful and apposite comments on the book in its various stages of gestation, almost all of which I have addressed or incorporated.

About the author

Jeremy Holmes, MD FRCPsych, was an NHS consultant psychiatrist, first in London and then in North Devon. Honorary professor at the University of Exeter, he co-founded the Exeter master's and now doctoral programme in psychoanalytic studies. He is author or co-author of more than twenty books and 250 papers, and lectures nationally and internationally. Now largely retired, he maintains a part-time private psychotherapy practice alongside grandparenting, allotment gardening, and green politics.

CHAPTER 1

Questions, questions ...

Sunday morning in early spring. We are silently sitting in the seventeenth-century Friends Meeting House in Hertford, UK, the oldest Quaker building in the country still in worshipful use. It is a large space, with oak beams still visible, although now safely buttressed by steel joists. The pews, likewise oak, while not quite bare ruined choirs, could not remotely be described as comfortable. None of our scant fellow communicants, perhaps half a dozen, including ourselves, is in the first flush of youth.

At first glance, a place of worship has no utilitarian value. Yet into these empty spaces, bounded, separated from the outside world, imbued either with silence, or with designated sounds—the muezzin's call to prayer, the swelling music of the organ, the ringing of Buddhist bells—emerges a distinctive presence.

I'm going to suggest that aspects of the psychotherapist's consulting room echo this absence/presence theme. But staying with the meeting house for now, I imagine my fellow participants sensing the invisible immanence of God—however that construct speaks to them. For me however, the predominant and poignant feeling is of painful *disenchantment*, Charles Taylor's (2007) epithet. I find myself inhabiting a deity-absent enclosure, a void, a vacuum. Resisting this insistent nihilism, I try to visualise this space not as void, but populated by a miraculous materiality, living and non-living. I picture the gases which make up its seeming emptiness populated with myriad microorganisms, our fellow inhabitants in this possibly unique life-speck in an infinite universe.

And now another horrible set of thoughts comes crowding in. Could there be a parallel between our worthy quasi-Quakerism, and my chosen occupation and veneration-object, psychoanalytic psychotherapy? Are we analytic therapists no more than theory-obsolete geriatrics, worshipping dead gods in an empty space, while the world rushes by, oblivious to our cherished practices and theories?

My answer, the starting point and conclusion of this book, is an insistent no! I argue that psychoanalytic psychotherapy can make a vital contribution to a healthy and emerging twenty-first-century culture, as well as being a necessary foil to the hegemony of the commodified, short-term, solutionistic therapies that are the prevailing psychotherapeutic genre.

The book's themes

Here then are some of the questions I try to address. Is there a space for the psychoanalytic spirit—and we shall be exploring what that might mean—to flourish in our current twenty-first-century context? Can recent advances in relational neuroscience inform and broaden psychoanalytic ideas and practices and even encompass psychoanalysis's 'spiritual' aspects? Is there a possible dialogue between psychoanalysis and the secular spirituality implicit in my clumsy glimpse into Spinozian sacred materialism (Damasio, 2004)? In the light of that, are there ways in which human–environment ecology can be brought into an equation that also encompasses psychotherapy?

With these big questions, inevitably, come commensurate doubts. Fools rush in. What could I possibly say that hasn't already been said, and in ways that are so much more scholarly and eloquent (e.g. Allen, 2022; Bion, 1990; Black, 2006, 2023; Eigen, 1998; Field, 2005; Fromm, 1986; Safran, 2003)? Yet to give up now would be ungrateful to those volunteers I've interviewed for this project, and indeed all the patients from whom I've learned in my generally happy working life in psychoanalytic psychiatry. Plus, behind that, there's an end-of-worklife itch, a niggle, something needs to be got off my chest.

But what on earth—or heaven—has a focus on 'spirit' to do with the everyday pragmatics of psychoanalytic psychotherapy? One of the guiding principles of my practice is, whenever possible, to steer clear of direct questions, which typically produce defensive or uninformative responses. What's always needed is a *story*. I ask my patients at the outset some version of the following: 'Let's think about what's led up to you finding yourself, at this point in your life, in this room, with this particular therapist-person.' Always there *is* a story, a life story, a path, familiar or less travelled. And behind that story there's always another. And another. So here goes.

For most of my working life I've been a hospital and clinic-based psychiatrist and psychoanalytic psychotherapist. In my practice and thinking I embraced the 'evidence-based' paradigm which dominates today's public discourse. I have resisted the idea of psychotherapy as a mystical or esoteric cultish realm, where belief rather than intellectual rigour and efficacious practice hold sway. I have championed the accumulating evidence showing that psychoanalytic therapies are equally if not more efficient and effective than pharmacological methods of treatment for many kinds of mental illness (e.g. Fonagy et al., 2015; Leichsenring, 2008; Shedler, 2010). I have championed the view that if psychotherapy is not to be the exclusive preserve of the comfortably off middle classes, all those with psychological ill-health deserve levels of 'third party' (i.e. state) funding comparable to those available for physical illnesses.

But here we come up against a number of problems. First, although we know that psychotherapy helps people to get 'better', it remains far from clear exactly how this comes about. Is it 'insight', 'accurate interpretation', challenge, task-setting and homework, the 'non-specific common factor' benefits of a guiding relationship (Wampold, 2015), acceptance, the passage of time and sense that 'this too will pass', 'intelligent kindness' (Ballatt et al., 2021)—compassionate love (Ferenczi, 1928) even? Is it meaningful to claim, as some have done (Pargament, 2007), that therapists are 'soul-healers', or should they better be seen as interpersonal technicians, akin to sports coaches, equipping their subjects with the skills needed better to negotiate the rough terrains of life? Or, taking an evolutionary perspective, can psychotherapy help its clients move from simplistic and often self-defeating relationships into a more complex and subtle stance vis-à-vis the interpersonal landscape that is our human milieu.

Therapy's overt social role is to help redress 'psychopathology'—psychosis, depression, anxiety, addictions, self-injury, eating disorders. Its aim is to make its subjects' lives more tolerable, to lessen self-injurious and self-defeating patterns, to foster more satisfying engagement with others, to help people value their strengths and accept their failings and limitations.

The social dimension

As conceived by modern medical psychotherapy, psychopathology is located within a suffering individual. But psychological symptoms are invariably nested in an existential, interpersonal, and social context. While emerging in the individual life-history, they manifest the complexity and vulnerability of life itself, and of the interpersonal and social relationships intrinsic to our species. In grossly unequal societies illness and social pathology go hand in hand (Marmot, 2016; Wilkinson & Pickett, 2009). Trauma, disease, dissolution, and premature death cluster among the disadvantaged and oppressed. Man-made degradations, cruelties, inequalities, and neglect prevail. Although their frequency can be lessened, their impact mitigated, the steep curve of their unequal distribution flattened, the reality of suffering, and of its social nature remains.

How does one confront indiscriminate randomness of existence—that, as it is sometimes put, bad things happen to good people (Kushner, 2004), and conversely perhaps, that 'bad' people often 'get away with it', largely unscathed? Why are the benefits and limitations of life so unequally distributed? How do we maintain hope in the face of the intractability and entrenchedness of much mental suffering? How do we find ways to live with the fact that our pristine selves and our loved ones are subject to trauma, illness, and loss? Given that all or most of our efforts are directed towards maintaining and perpetuating life, how do we encompass the inescapability of death? How do we come to terms with knowing that we will inevitably sometimes hurt and be hurt by those whom we love? What is our 'place' in the world, and how do we make sense of it? What is the overall story we tell ourselves about our life, its direction and meaning? In one way or another, these existential themes permeate psychotherapeutic work, yet are signally not captured by the evidence-based paradigm, by cognitive and behavioural therapy (CBT) protocols or even simplistic psychoanalytic formulae (cf. Van Deurzen & Kenward, 2005; Yalom, 1980).

A related problematic is the role of the environment in relation to psychotherapy. Scientific medicine has progressed from van Leeuwenhoek's microscope to the miracles of modern molecular genetics. This has come about by an extraordinary focus, in William Blake's phrase, on the 'minute particulars' of biological reality. But despite a less audible drum roll, medical science has also advanced with equal success through the wide-angle vision of public health. Jenner's vaccination saved thousands of lives 150 years before the variola virus was identified. The world's recovery from the Covid-19 pandemic was achieved by virology and public health working hand-in-hand.

In psychotherapy, the 'setting'—a comfortable chair or couch, warmth, quietness, regularity, receptive attention—provides the equivalent of physical medicine's microscopy, enabling the structure and content of lived experience to be scrutinised without distraction. Relational neuroscience is the psychotherapeutic analogue of molecular genetics. But, with notable exceptions (Bowlby, 1971; Fromm, 1973; Hopper, 2012), psychotherapists have downplayed the role of the environment no less than in physical medicine. An implicit assumption is that, once agency and self-understanding are instated or reinstated, people will choose to love and work and create in less adverse circumstances than those which brought them for help.

Returning to an unchanged environment often means that the gains of therapy gradually unravel. For the poor and/or emotionally deprived, those environments are often inexorable in their grinding immutability. Despite the contributions of family therapy and the now sadly near-defunct therapeutic community movement, the wider *context* of patients' lives has, until recently, been largely ignored by psychotherapy. As one patient said—his father had been killed in the Second World War with disastrous consequences for his upbringing—neatly standing Spike Milligan's famous epigram on its head, 'Hitler, his part in my downfall'. This ecological dimension—which I shall argue includes religious and/or spiritual aspects—remains largely unacknowledged and untheorised. Our relationship with social forces beyond the family, including the physical and natural world, and the health-giving properties of connectedness and shared affect, are areas which psychotherapists are only just beginning to address (Music, 2014; Stuart-Smith, 2020).

Psychotherapy for whom?

Another largely silent zone in psychotherapeutic discourse concerns a built-in tension in the ethics of psychotherapy provision. Should it follow utilitarian triage-ism, aiming to reduce the greatest amount of unhappiness for the greatest number of people? This, in the UK, has translated into providing a strictly limited number of sessions of CBT for all deemed likely to benefit from it (Layard & Clark, 2014). Or should the 'virtue ethics' project, which sees each life as uniquely valuable, hold sway? The latter might entail investing in prolonged and intense psychoanalytic work in order to maximise the individual's psychological health, comparable to the costly and prolonged treatment deemed necessary to support those suffering from chronic physical illnesses such as cystic fibrosis, kidney failure, complex heart disease, or diabetes. A handful of countries acknowledge this—Germany, Austria, Australia, Canada—and subsidise long-term psychoanalytic psychotherapy, but for the most part it is left to the private sector to provide such intensive care, and therefore, scandalously, to exclude those most in need.

As with the UK National Health Service, and these exceptional examples of state funded psychoanalysis, religious 'services' are 'free at the point of need'. But, like psychotherapy and psychotherapists, in the end they have to be paid for. Priests and imams must eat, churches and mosques maintained. Both Judaism and Islam carry the expectation that their adherents will donate a significant percentage (typically 2.5%) of their income to charity. But, unlike in psychotherapy, there is no individual financial contract with a priest, even though there may be general non-financial expectations such at attendance at services, wearing religious insignia, etc.

Even at the everyday pragmatic level there are implications of these themes—existential, social, and ethical—for the practising psychotherapist. Spiritual or religious life, formal or informal, plays a significant part in many people's psychology. I worked for a while as a therapist attached to a counselling service for clergy, a group no less susceptible to psychological illness than other occupations. Here the basic principles of practice entailed maintaining a strictly non-judgemental and accepting position vis-à-vis another's worldview, and the willingness to learn from my clergy clients about religion, whichever version of Christianity—'high' Anglican, evangelical, or all points between—they happened to espouse. I worked from the position that seeing a person's relationship to God or gods is comparable to their relationship with other significant figures in their life, and therapy entailed finding ways to include them in our conversations. I would often find myself pondering out loud such thoughts as 'Can we think about what God might make of your depression?'

Overall, despite my own—and here revealed—agnostically atheistic viewpoint, and the intrinsically secular role of the physician, vis-à-vis my patients I try to abide by the Yeatsean principle and assume that my patients want me to: 'Tread softly because you tread on my dreams' (Yeats, 1899). This is not far removed from the general rule that it is never a good idea to criticise one's friends' children or pets—however irritating they may be. People's cherished beliefs need to be treated with the utmost respect. Failing to do so invariably evokes defensiveness and a diminution of trust.

Agency

To continue in this 'beyond evidence-based practice' vein, another crucial existential theme is that of *agency*—the move from thought and intention to action. Dante's midlife crisis *Divine Comedy* protagonist needed his fellow poet Virgil to guide him through Hell and then Purgatory in his search for love and salvation. Psychotherapy too can be thought of as a journey in which patients draw on therapists' familiarity with the territory and the terrors of the inner world to help them in their quest. But, as with Dante's hero's panic as he approached Paradise, knowing that pre-Christian Virgil could no longer accompany him beyond Purgatory and towards his beloved Beatrice, there comes a point when, for all the therapist's good intentions, the patient is on her or his own.

Restoring the capacity for choice, autonomy, and agency—replacing *outrage*, however justified, with improved but imperfect *outcome*—is a central benefit of therapy. By definition, autonomy and choice, and the courage they entail, can only be made for oneself. As Marx famously put it, 'philosophers have only interpreted the world in various ways; the point however is to change it' (Marx & Engels, 1844). In the end, psychotherapy patients have to draw on the understandings and relational transformations of therapy for themselves if they are to modify their lives for the better.

Existential themes

An accompanying existential theme is the irreversibility of time. No amount of therapy can bring back a lost loved one, or undo the pain and misery wrought by neglect, abuse, and adversity. But although the facts of the past cannot be altered, their context and impact on present experience can. We constantly rewrite history, revising the past in the light of the present (in psychoanalytic jargon, *'Nachträglichkeit'*, *'après coup'*, or 'afterwardness'), and the present in the light of the past. Helping patients to face, mourn, and transcend their injuries, failures, and limitations, and to see them as inescapable facts of life is built into the psychotherapeutic project.

> Ben sought help with the guilt he was suffering about the impact on his children and ex-wife of leaving his unsatisfactory marriage and establishing a more satisfying and stimulating new relationship.
>
> Sexually abused by his father as a child, he had played a part in his eventual imprisonment. Therapy focused on the confusion in Ben's mind between the guilt he felt about this betrayal, and the misery he felt the break-up of the family was inflicting upon his children—despite the fact that they appeared to be coping well with their parents' separation and shared care arrangements.
>
> When the end of this time-limited therapy approached, Ben said the intervention that had been most helpful was the therapist's contention that impermanence is as much a fact of life as are connection and attachment, and her comment that the fragility

of marriage, whether due to forced migration, death, or divorce, alongside maturation and mistakes, is a sad but universal truth from which none are fully immune.

These existential themes—how to lead a good life, how to come to terms with illness, pain, and death, how to find meaning of the world into which we find ourselves 'thrown'—are traditionally the province of religion. But 'we' WEIRDos—Western, Educated, Industrialised, Rich, Democratic (Henrich, 2021)—whether atheistic, formally religious, or vaguely 'spiritual', have to come to terms with 'disenchantment', and the fact that, like it or not, we live in a largely secular age. This secularism can be seen as one facet of the ongoing Enlightenment project, which values truth, evidence, and universalism (Neiman, 2016). The purpose of this book is to explore the extent to which psychotherapy has come to occupy some of the territory previously occupied by religion, the ways in which this might be so, and the implications for psychotherapy practice. I write not in the spirit of debunking psychoanalytic psychotherapy and viewing it as a 'mere' species of religion (cf. Epstein, 2006), but rather to recognise the ubiquity, history, and strengths of religion, and how psychotherapy might draw on this legacy and extend and deepen it. Nevertheless, one might consider the counter-factual or hypothetical question: if therapy were a species of religion, what sort of religion might it be? In what follows I explore some of the ramifications of this. I realise that even to ask such a question may raise the hackles of those aiming to establish the validity and indispensability of our discipline in a secular world. To them I beg a degree of 'negative capability' or at least benefit of the doubt. Far from wanting to discredit psychotherapy, my hope is to extend its scope beyond a still shaky evidence-based practice, and to validate more fully its cultural presence.

Caveats

Before embarking, three further warnings and anticipatory apologies are required. First, although I am deeply interested in the role religion plays in people's lives, and have made auto-didactic efforts to follow the literature on the spirituality–psychotherapy interface, it is evident that I am a theological sophomore. In the peer review feedback on the proposal for this book, one reviewer, clearly irritated by my theological naïvety, picked up on this. Initially I was mildly mortified, but then found myself thinking how I might have responded similarly if sent a book by a clergyman pontificating about psychotherapy.

A second, self-evident disclaimer is that I adopt an unashamed ecumenical stance, both theologically and psychotherapeutically. I transition, as do my subjects, in a frictionless way between the Abrahamic religions, as well as Druidism, Buddhism, and—my own favoured position—a species of eco-agnosticism. Equally, I have not concerned myself greatly with the differences between the major sub-groups of psychoanalytic psychotherapy—psychoanalytic, Jungian, self-psychological, attachment-informed, relational, etc. I follow the Wampold (2015) view that the similarities between the psychotherapies far outweigh their differences, and that, for example, CBT therapists often fly under flags of convenience and funding while in truth their relational competence offers something much more akin to psychoanalytic psychotherapy—the same being true, perhaps to a lesser extent, vice versa.

A third apologia: the text is broken up throughout with illustrative case vignettes. All are 'true fictions' in the sense that, while 'made up', they are based on real-life clinical work, or the interviews which form the basis of Chapter 6. Confidentiality is a tortured and problematic aspect of psychotherapeutic writing, but I sincerely hope to have conformed to ethical guidelines, caused no injury or offence, while remaining faithful to clinical reality.

CHAPTER 2

Starting points: summary of the book's main arguments

The notion of spirituality is by its nature an abstraction, a sublimation, a distillation of everyday experience. Likewise, this chapter attempts to explicate the book's essence. It arises out of a juxtaposition of two frameworks, one contemporary, one firmly embedded in the psychoanalytic canon. The first is the 'free energy principle' developed by the mathematician-psychiatrist Karl Friston and his colleagues (Friston, 2010; Friston et al., 2018; Seth, 2022) and which has been applied to the processes of psychotherapy, among others, by Cahart-Harris and Friston (2019), Solms (2021), and Holmes (2020). The second is the Winnicottian concept of 'transitional space', which I shall argue is the locus for higher levels of shared/relational free energy minimising.

As with our new patient laying out their story, I ask readers temporarily to suspend disbelief—and belief—and to accept the rough contours of my argument, in the hope that later chapters will make things clearer and more convincing. Or—yet perish the thought—another option, for those determinedly allergic to neuroscience, is to skip, and move briskly on to the next chapter.

My starting point is the contention that, in the Global North at least, psychotherapy occupies a specific and necessary psychological and social role in an age of formal religious decline and pervasive 'disenchantment'. Psychotherapy and counselling are custodians of the inner life in ways previously occupied by religion. The consulting room parallels a church as a place of safety in an uncertain and trauma-stalked world. I'm suggesting that the ethos of psychotherapy is one of *secular spirituality*, the essence of which is connectedness, interpersonally with our fellow humans, but also with the living and non-living entities whose existence we share.

This concurrence of psychotherapy and spirituality arises at a fundamental biological level from the fact that we live in a world of *radical uncertainty*. Our knowledge of ourselves, of others, and of what is to come is inescapably constrained. We are limited by the *veil of ignorance* drawn by the narrow range of our senses, by the fact that the brain is only statistically rather directly connected with the surrounding 'world', by time's unidirectional arrow, and by the tendency towards *entropy/disorder*, which the second law of thermodynamics tells us is, where 'we'—our selves, our species, our planet, and our universe—are in the short and long runs heading.

Friston and free energy

Current neuroscience (e.g. Seth, 2022) holds that, like all living creatures, we negotiate this uncertainty by making *Bayesian predictions*, based on prior experience and current sensory information about the likely state of the world and imagined consequences of our actions. This Bayesianism is embedded in the wider context of the need to stave off entropy—for a while at least. In order to survive and thrive, an organism must minimise the disruptive forces with which it is beset. Life depends on order and the maintenance of boundaries, the very antithesis of entropic chaos. As quantum physicist Erwin Schrödinger (1944), asking himself '*What is life?*', succinctly put it, life is 'negentropy'.

And for motile organisms, that is, the animal kingdom, this is where brains—their own and those of their conspecifics—come in. Brains integrate and regulate incoming information about the state of the world and the inner state of the organism itself. They do this, as best they can, by *minimising free energy* (Friston, 2010, 2018). Energy here refers to informational energy: order is high in energy, disorder low. A fuzzy TV screen tells us 'nothing' and thus is high in entropy. A low entropy crisp picture represents free energy channelled and minimised, giving us needed information, from the triviality of football scores to a heart-stopping Middle-Eastern death toll.

The idea of free energy minimisation (FEM), like heliocentrism, is counter-intuitive. As Wittgenstein said, why would one *not* think the sun went round the earth. Similarly, *pace* Isherwood (1939), it is surprising to think that we are *not* cameras, reproducing a pristine vision of 'the world' derived from the senses and registered or represented in the cerebral cortex. In reality, we see not with our eyes, but our minds; our versions of the world around us are more akin to testable illusions than pixelated reproductions (Hoffman, 2019). Based on prior experience, we have built up pre-existing pictures of 'our' world and its *affordances* (Gibson, 1986), that is, those features which 'matter' to us, for survival, security, pleasure, reproduction, etc. We—our brains— continuously compare and correlate our working models of the world, 'top-down', with incoming information, as derived 'bottom-up' from our senses. Where there is correspondence, the incoming sensory information/energy is 'bound' and can be taken for granted. Attention is alerted by and focuses on discrepancies/anomalies, which in turn trigger minor or major readjustments of our preformed models of 'reality'. The reason that Leonardo's *Mona Lisa* continues to excite admiration and wonder half a millennium after it was painted rests with the enigmatic, and so attention-grabbing 'smile'—is it invitation, modest rejection, denoting satisfaction or concealed misery?

To repeat, incoming 'free energy', generated bottom-up by the senses, is chaotic and 'unbound'. Brains, top-down, 'bind' and so minimise free energy with their preformed models of what they predict, Bayes-wise, the world is likely to be like. This occurs hierarchically from level to level within the brain, from sense organs 'upwards' to the higher reaches of consciousness. At each stage residual discrepancies between incoming sensory information and preformed models are passed upwards for further minimisation. Unbound free energy eventually (although we're talking milliseconds here) is passed to the prefrontal cortex with its capacity for conscious thinking, and, crucially from a psychotherapeutic perspective, for thinking about thinking, adding another potentially health-giving top-down layer to the hierarchy.

This goes on continuously and dynamically in a loop which includes sensation, FEM, and action, stimulating further sensation, as the world changes in consequence of action, and so on. Thus once a 'situation' is appraised—which may happen entirely below consciousness at a purely physiological level—action (including speech, which is a form of action) follows, consciously directed or otherwise.

From the brain's point of view, free energy arises out of the discrepancy between its models of the world and the incoming information provided by the senses. The upper limit of free energy is 'surprisal', which equates, once again, to chaos and entropy. The principle of homeostasis, on which our survival depends, insists that free energy/surprisal is required to be minimised by all means possible.

Under the aegis of the free energy principle, we adaptively align ourselves and our top-down models with the state of play of the world— inner and outer—as we perceive it. This alignment is achieved in three main ways. We *act* so as to enhance the *precision of perceptions*, for example looking yet more closely at *La Giaconda*; second, on the basis of this *generating modified models* that correspond with the world-as-it-appears. Here surprisal is embraced and used to stimulate *creative adaptation*. A third strategy, seen often in psychopathology, is to *move into and create environments* where the contours of reality are constrained in ways *that correspond with our pre-existing models*. Thus do we create the very 'world' which we expect. In a psychotherapy setting this forms the basis of transference and projective identification.

As suggested, permeating this model of brain function is the notion of *Bayesian inference*. With no direct access to the world, external and internal, other than that provided by our limited and often erroneous senses, we speculate about its present and future states. These informed guesses or predictions will be guided by a combination of past experience and current input and modified accordingly by our actions. We've yet to see the sun rise in the west and so it's a safe bet that it won't tomorrow, and so we can direct our strictly limited attention and energy elsewhere, although of course for a newborn on the first day of their life, this would not be so.

Let's return to the hierarchical nature of bottom-up/top-down surprise minimisation. As information ascends the minimisation ladder, so specificity increases: round object/mouth-and-eyes/human/male/mid-fifties/in contextually known dwelling—can be no one else but my brother. At each step along the way *surplus uncertainty* is passed up to the next level where the relevant repertoire of top-down models is deployed until a statistical best fit is found. It is only at this point that consciousness supervenes in this these self-sustaining neuronal processes.

And here one can add another layer, often unconscious, that is of vital relevance to psychotherapy. Because the process is probabilistic, allowance must be made for error. After all, my perception—although perhaps better thought of as a *perceptive construction*—might be wrong. Perhaps that's just someone who *looks like* my brother. And, what's more, maybe I just *wanted* him to turn out to be my brother, because I haven't seen him for ages. In this sense unconscious perception is wish-fulfilment—in broad daylight, not just in our dreams. To counter-act this, where id was, there ego shall, and, for survival purposes must, be. Beyond the top level of my model-making there is a need for another layer in which the very assumptions I deploy are questioned, and the possibilities of wish-mediated error, or indeed the inescapable 'noise' of a subject-to-error sense organ, taken into account. That might be my brother—how I wish it was—but, equally, it could be his double; let's get more information to minimise error and resolve the question. In these neuroscience terms, my surprise-minimisation apparatus needs to include a self-referential or 'mentalizing' aspect which takes my wishes, and how they may shape my perceptions, into account. These in turn stimulate error minimising strategies—for example, taking a closer look at the putative brother, and, as we shall see, asking my *companion* if he/she recognises that person.

Examining these wish-driven constructs are the familiar territory of psychoanalytic psychotherapy. The ambiguous persona of the self-effacing therapist brings to light clients' assumptions, revealing their Bayesian store of past experience-based assumptions. Becoming con-scious of these unconscious processes adds another layer to the hier-archical surprise-minimising millefeuille. This *thinking about thinking* gives subjects greater understanding of their world and actions, which in turn enhances their likelihood of more skilful living. This is espe-cially applicable to attachment-oriented psychotherapy with its empha-sis on self-reflexive function or mentalizing.

How does this perhaps arcane-seeming neuroscience relate to our target topic of psychotherapy and spirituality? The kernel of my argument is that in any real-life 'present moment' there is always a quantum of *unminimised free energy* with which the mind/brain has to contend—and/or creatively develop—but which remains beyond the reach of minimisation manoeuvres. Our knowledge of the world, and the world as it exists are never fully in kilter. Let's call this area of *necessary uncertainty* the realm of 'spirit'—a form of life in a living brain, but life that cannot readily be formulated, represented, or regulated. This arena of uncertainty is where psychotherapy and spirituality overlap, both wrestling with the same source of knowing and unknowing.

The paradox of unminimised free energy is that attempts to embody and encapsulate it—through practice, gesture, speech, or silence—are confounded by its very essence. There is always superfluity, energy that remains confoundingly unbound. Our models of the world can never fully comprehend its full complexity. Acknowledgement of this uncertainty underlies the 'negative capability' inherent in the reverie-driven psychoanalytic psychotherapy stance of authors such as Bion (1990), Ferro (Civitarese & Ferro, 2022), and Ogden (2016) and to which I too subscribe (Holmes & Storr, 2024). We cannot fully impose order, yet cannot not try, and in the attempt miss the unknowability of a reality that is ever beyond our reach.

There are many ways of attempting to quell the discomfort this evokes. One can put one's *trust* in a loving God, the very word implying the need for a 'leap of faith' over the abyss of radical uncertainty. In the face of glimpses of entropy one can console oneself with passing it along to a deity: 'that's God's business'. Like Wittgenstein, one can invoke a kind of logic-driven awe: 'whereof one cannot speak, thereof one must be silent'. In medieval times it was held that angels, by definition invisible, could become manifest by clothing themselves in air, famously expressed in Donne's 'Air and angels' poem (Donne, 2006). This brought their mysteries down to earth, as, when faced with existential challenge, do the conversations of consulting room or cloister.

Winnicott and transitionality

Humans are hyper-social creatures. We are evolutionarily endowed not with speed or strength but with big brains—and, relatedly, each other. In the search for FEM we recruit and rely on others, with whom we form, in Friston and Frith's (2015) phrase, 'duets for one', or as Bateman (2022) puts it, we enter into mentalizing or 'we-mode'. This is a process which has significant mental health implications, given that, when it comes to reality modelling, two heads are generally better than one. Thus the focus of mentalization based therapy (MBT) is to help suicidal and relationally dysfunctional clients move from lone 'I-mode' and 'me-mode' thinking and feeling to 'we-mode' collaborative mentalizing. The therapist's words and gestures, and her client's parallel responses, are the bridges that connect one brain to another.

The fabric of religious praxis—text, chant, song, and sign-making—similarly creates a free energy-binding chorus at a group rather than dyadic level, and in a general rather than individualised way. With the help of therapy or religion, we *make sense* of the world, thereby creating top-down, energy-binding order out of the unbound free energy with which our senses and ever-renewing life experiences threaten to flood us.

What I am calling 'transitionality' or we-mode is thus:

a) Interpersonal;
b) Neither 'phantasy' nor 'reality' but pertains to both;
c) Imaginative, hypothetical, playful;
d) Free energy-binding;
e) The birthplace of religious belief/ideology, and psychoanalytic interpretation/formulation.

Transitionality opens up a virtual space where neither the constraints of reality nor the madness of dreams prevails. Hypothetical possibilities for action can be rehearsed, affect co-regulated and so yoked to cognition. Impulses can be strengthened or discarded. But the psychotherapy patient is epistemically challenged (Fonagy & Allison, 2014). Her transitional space is constricted. She doesn't know who or what to trust. Her trauma-formed models of the world do not steer her safely through life's rocky passages. She is either painfully pressed against an unyielding reality, or trapped in the shadows of her tormented inner world, with no thinking space between 'is' (the concrete reality of trauma) and 'aught' (wishes, hopes, and imaginings that things could have been and could be different).

Note too that those in positions of power—priests, parents, or politicians—may evade transitionality and directly constrain others to behave as their predictions and preformed worldview require. Their own free energy is thereby minimised by exporting it to those in their thrall. Their negentropy rests at the expense of others, at a controlling or even sadomasochistic price. The poor live shorter lives than the rich: the spirit level is highly uneven (Wilkinson & Pickett, 2009). The origins of this can be seen in infancy and childhood where the roots of personality and psychopathology are laid down, and where socio-economic stress pushes up the incidence of insecure attachment, where the need for short-term survival outweighs relational resilience.

Psychotherapy helps redress these limitations on transitionality in a number of ways. First, a zone of safety is created where uncertainty is seen as legitimate, expectable, and face-able. Second, it is a shared, interpersonal *holding area* where therapist and patient coexist, collaborate, and form a viable 'duet for one'. Third, this zone is 'transitional', a play space neither wholly 'real' nor fully permeated with phantasy. Fourth, the therapist, on the basis of countertransference, makes conjectural interpretations in which the pain of uncertainty and the need for defences against it are acknowledged. Fifth, it provides an imaginative workshop in which new models of the world, bypassing repression and thus better able to encompass a client's 'downloads' of the world and her associations thereto and thus to bind free energy, are co-created. Finally, via transference, it provides a top-down, meta-view of one's self and one's self-in-relation-to-others, one's strengths and limitations. This in turn enables the psychotherapy subject to engage with uncertainty—energy unbound—redressing the free-energy paradox by helping the unknown to be accepted in all its unknown-ness.

Apropos, Freud (1919h) was fascinated by the 'Uncanny', by the bizarreness of dreams and by the seemingly perverse and self-undermining workings of the unconscious. By contrast, the free energy perspective sees the workings of 'the unconscious' as adaptive: attempts, via avoidance, repression, splitting, and/or coercive interpersonal behaviours, however limiting or self-defeating these may prove to be in the longer term, to minimise free energy. The self–world discrepancies of psychosis are manifestations of energy binding gone awry. Paranoia or psychotic delusions, as Freud once put it, can be thought of as patches on a rent in the ego, top-down attempts to minimise free energy, even at the expense of gross misapprehensions of reality. Likewise, contemporary neuroscience sees dream work not as manifestations of repression (disguised wishes), but as mental 'housekeeping', sifting through the 'day's residues', discarding the irrelevant, consolidating existing models of the world, and generating new stories ready to encompass dangers as yet unmet.

How do religion and spirituality fit in with this model? My argument is that the experiential realm of spirituality, like that of psychotherapy, represents an attempt to tackle the problem of energy unbound. We try never to be alone with free energy. What's feared can, with the help of others, be faced, transcended, and lived with. The religious community—in Buddhist terms 'the sanga'—is an essential part of religion's answer to our problem of living in an uncertain, unpredictable, and ultimately unknowable world. We 'borrow' one another's brains, create a combined chorus, and thereby come up with creative solutions to our free energy problems, simplistic or sophisticated. This includes acknowledgement that entropy, in the form of death as life's counterpoint, will in the end win—and necessarily so. Evolution depends on death-cleared decks so that new life can begin again. Were eternity possible, it would be the recurring cycle of life, death, and new life.

Intrinsic to spirituality is community, connections to like-minded others with whom uncertainty can be shared and free energy minimised. Religious and spiritual ideas and ideologies are top-down models that have free energy built-in. A god simultaneously encompasses, and minimises the free energy out of which he/she is fashioned. Knowing and unknowing are co-yoked. Phoenix-like, the Hindu goddess Kali embodies the fires of creative destruction. In Abrahamic religions, God is both an omnipresent friend and moves in mysterious ways. Milton's Satan, another creative and likeable destroyer, is a fallen angel. In Buddhism, suffering—the affective pain of free energy—is integral to our existence. If pantheistic, or pan-entheistic, our ecological embeddedness is never stable, given that planetary conditions are ever-changing and our models of the world never quite catch up with this cyclicity. Spirituality thus supervenes free energy with concepts that are themselves coloured by it.

The social role of psychotherapy

But Winnicottian transitionality and 'we-goism' are in short supply. In our Western, individualised, secularised world collective ties, the villages that it takes to raise children, have weakened. Unlike our hunter-gatherer forebears, we no longer share a common niche. Class, ethnicity, skin colour, wealth, education, migration, capital, appropriation, and consumerism confine us to our individual thought-boxes, silos, and echo-chambers. The gulfs between us—especially between haves and have-nots—is ever widening. All around us swirls free energy demanding collective supra-organismal binding.

This need is to an extent met by our political and ethnic and religious affiliations and identifications. Here too we seek help from many sources, including, via social media support groups, our fellow sufferers—but also the new priesthood of counsellors and therapists. If lucky, we form a 'duet for one' with a therapist, individually or in a group. Because it is our free energy, not hers, our therapist can help us face, name, and trace the anachronisms of our pre-existing models, and delineate the ways in which they lie at the root of our depression, anxiety, or psychosis. If things go well, we learn to develop more sophisticated working models with which to bind free energy. Psychotherapy raises our spirits.

For all this to happen a psychotherapy-defined zone is needed. This is no less than Winnicottian transitional space. Its boundaries are clear: at one end is the internal world, teeming with memories, comforting and/or traumatic, and established top-down pathways with which we shape our worlds. At the other limit stands brute reality, internal and external. Here we are pressed against the physics and chemistry of our physiology, and the social and political ecology into which fate has arbitrarily thrown us. Therapeutic and/or spiritual relatedness opens up the shared transitional space between these two bookends. Here flourish dreams, creativity, and imaginings pointing to new possibilities. Transitionality is where we live, and where we feel most alive. Our psychic thriving and surviving depends on how we negotiate the space between these two poles. This is what I am calling a spiritual zone—and also where psychotherapy feels most at home.

The role of the metaphorically held hand of a therapist or spiritual companion enables its subjects to make use of this transitional space. Free energy is jointly bound. Terror transforms into surprise, jitters into jouissance. Spontaneity supervenes over mere survival. New formulations of one's life, one's confusions, one's injuries—inflicted and suffered—emerge. Eventually the external shared space becomes internalised, no longer dependent on the continuing presence of the therapist. For some, a more religiously inflected spirituality may take over where psychotherapy left off. God—or nature—now become the dialogic other. There is genuine healing, never completed perhaps, but no longer despaired of.

This spiritual angle on therapy has practical implications. First, at the intangible peripheries of therapy there is always a degree of uncertainty which calls to be acknowledged. Immutable psychotherapeutic truths are eschewed. As therapists we try to shine light into a psychic abyss. Our formulations make sense of things, but they are, in the end, no more than words and theories of our own and our discipline's weavings, themselves subject to the vagaries of free energy. The psychotherapeutic map can never be the territory. Our interventions, even if boldly delivered for clients in states of confusion, will nevertheless be hedged around with degrees of tentativeness and due modesty.

Second, therapeutic space is one where the totality of the trouble-related thoughts of both client and therapist can safely be contained. Each and every free association on the client's part belongs there, as do the panoply of countertransference reactions of the therapist. These are 'unbound' in the sense that they arise spontaneously and cannot be legislated for by any psychotherapy textbook. This leads to a third principle: the democratic parity of client and therapist. Their voices are equal. Neither is intrinsically privileged, despite their very differing roles in the consulting room. The attachment-derived concept of mentalizing captures some of this democratic drive—the idea that each individual has her unique projects, desires, and perspectives. The irony of mentalizing is that it starts from the essential unknowability of others, and therefore respect for their spiritual autonomy. The therapist tries to understand her client, but knows that she will never fully succeed. The hope is that clients will gradually become equipped with their own mentalizing capacities and so better able to know and understand themselves and to negotiate the vicissitudes of relational life.

This perspective, with its built-in uncertainty, differentiates spiritual psychotherapy from life-coaching, management, and workplace supervision. The therapist has no 'agenda', hidden or otherwise, other than mutually to explore with the client (which may also be an organisation or subgroup thereof) 'what's going on', and to give voice to the thoughts and feelings with which they struggle. Clients' free energy prior to consulting room examination either threatens with chaos or is subject to rigid suppression. The therapist unearths this unbound energy, holds it up to the light, so that it can be better bound and so harnessed to drive new patterns of living. In this the therapist adopts a position of 'non-attachment', not in the sense of avoidance or dismissal of affect, but as a hovering meta-level where the higher reaches of the hierarchy of FEM can be encountered and addressed.

This brings us to another aspect of spiritually informed therapy. Therapy at a deep level needs to be taken on trust. The psychotherapist and her techniques offer no guarantees. Solutions will be sought and sometimes found, however obscure or inaccessible these may at times seem. In psychodynamic terms, this basic trust reflects infants' trust in caregivers who will respond in a timely way to their needs, keep them safe, and celebrate their unique aliveness—some or all of which may have been compromised in their developmental history.

A final dimension of the spiritual aspect of psychotherapy concerns its position in society. Like religion, especially if 'unestablished', what goes on in consulting rooms is only partially within the purview of social control. The caring professions generally, and especially psycho-analytic psychotherapy, cannot be fully commodified. They stand or fall by their use-value rather than their exchange-value. How is one to tell what a session is 'worth', whether a £20 per hour e-counsellor gives different value to a £150 fully couched-up analyst—or crying on the shoulder of a sympathetic friend, or a prayerful church meeting?

There are ways of 'regulating' the profession, and good reasons for doing so as to protect naïve and vulnerable clients from financial or sexual exploitation. In the UK at least, psychotherapy regulation is self-regulation, other than the primary professional regulations of its practitioners. Perhaps it is right that this be so. The presence of Church of England bishops as members of the UK legislature gives spirituality of sorts a platform, but one that is compromised, perhaps fatally.

Whether regulated or not, psychotherapy's social role remains that of the partial outsider. It occupies a space, adjacent to, but not fully within the neo-liberal canon of capitalist exchange. It shares this ambiguity with other important but invisible, undervalued, and under-paid 'maternalistic' caring activities—child-rearing, care of the sick and elderly, youth sports coaching, various forms of voluntary social work, etc.

A core value for psychotherapy, shared with most religious and spiritual groups, but counter-cultural in the Western world, is that of bedrock relationality and interconnectedness (Dunbar, 2022). This is the 'groupness' or 'we-go' of our existence as opposed to ideologies based on genetic determinism, the hollow sovereignty of 'individual choice', or leader-worshipping populism. The secular spirituality of psychotherapy is salient to our world's predicament of climate change and ecological degradation. Through the praxis of borrowed brains, and the ethic of immanence—the sacredness of the everyday—psychotherapy has the potential to be a cultural beacon. In the FEM principle, a fish or aquatic mammal *in* water is a mirror or imprint of its environment. By contrast, a fish *out* of water is flooded with free energy, a world for which its mirror neurons have no counterpart, sensory input for which it has no model or coherent behavioural response.

Psychotherapy points to ways of living both with the human and non-human world that more closely align with their realties, and to a less entropic and more complexity-coherent future. But our times are out of joint; we are fish out of our environmental equilibrium. Spiritually informed psychotherapy and its offshoots are part of a wider movement to help the beached whale of humanity back where it belongs and longs, often unawares, to return.

CHAPTER 3

The difficulty of definitions

The principle of 'transitionality' discussed in the previous chapter is based on the observation that there is an intermediate zone between a 'fact' as it applies to the external world, and provisional thoughts or imaginative hypotheses about that world as they arise in the evolution-shaped human brain. The concepts we use to navigate our world are therefore often fuzzy and ill-defined. The aim of this chapter is to explore the ambiguity inherent in some of the recurring terms that are already shaping our discussion.

Spirituality

Spirituality is notoriously difficult to define, and especially to differentiate from its near neighbours, religion and theism. Struggling with this, I was relieved to discover the following (Vaillant, 2009, p. 4):

> Recently, I tentatively began to discuss spirituality with a close friend of mine, a brilliant woman *and a devout Anglican*. 'When I hear the word spirituality,' she exploded, 'I break out in spots!' (italics added)

Valliant's friend's dermatological eruptions are, it seems, reactions to the misuse of a word that for her had specific Christian meaning, but which has widened to encompass everything from faith healing and vague mysticism to various forms of 'covert narcissism'. Conversely, from a secular perspective, 'spirituality' can crop up as a weasel word, adding little to the notion of the psychological, and in its reified forms is essentially anti-psychological, or even perhaps devoid of any useful meaning. One of my aims here is to counter at least some of these reservations.

Spirituality's etymology derives from the notion of the breath, as in 'in*spir*ation', with its dual reference both to the bodily act of re*spir*ation, and the idea of being imbued with positive, creative, 'a*spir*ational' qualities that transcend the material self.

For Freud, this move from the physicality of breathing to the 'intellectual' notion of spirituality represents a significant cognitive advance:

> ... it was movements of the air that provided the prototype of intellectuality [*Geistigkeit*], for intellect [*Geist*] derives its name from a breath of wind—animus, spiritus, and the Hebrew ruach (breath) ... this led to the discovery of the mind [*Seele* (soul)]. (Freud, 1939a, p. 120)

There is a crucial point here that will colour our later discussion. For Freud, the transition from the physical and literal to the metaphysical—'intellectual' as he puts it—represented an important advance, paralleling the move from localised polytheism to the panoptic monotheism of the Abrahamic religions as they began to take hold on scattered semitic tribes. It also lies behind his notion of 'sublimation' as a psychologically healthy way of channelling sexual and aggressive drives. In contrast, I shall argue that the secular spirituality embodied in psychotherapy celebrates the particular, the embodied, the concrete praxis of the here-and-now, as against intellectual generalisation and abstraction. Behind this contrast lies the differences which Gilligan (2011) has described between 'masculine' and 'feminine' (often not gender-confined) discourse styles, Freud's abstract, authoritative prose epitomising the former, while specificity, self-referentiality, and vividness typify the latter.

In a pre-scientific age, the 'breath of life' referred to something that was invisible yet palpably integral to animate existence. The 'spirit' in this dualistic pre-physiological sense appeared to be the ethereal essence of life, inaccessible to anatomists: that of which a material body was emptied when it 'gave up the ghost'. The confusion and concrete thinking which the notion of 'spirituality' can arouse in the interface between the pre-scientific and scientific era is illustrated by MacDougall's notorious attempt to weigh the 'soul' at the moment of the death. This heroic pseudo-scientist claimed that, unlike supposedly soul-less dogs, the human body loses on average 20 grams in weight when body and spirit go their separate ways (Hood, 2009)—due, we subsequentially know, to the more rapid evaporation of fluid from the comparatively hairless human body in contrast to his hirsute best friend.

A gas of course is no less material than the muscles and bones which propel it to and from the lungs, and is equally subject to the laws of fluid mechanics that are palpable objects to the force of gravity and laws of Newtonian motion. Indeed, Newton's scientific precocity revealed itself at an early age when he was found in a field during a storm, proving to himself the materiality of air by discovering that he could jump two yards further with the wind behind him than against it (Gleik, 2004).

Spirituality, an abstract noun, is linked with the idea of the 'invisible'. Our consciousness excludes that which we cannot see, or, turning a blind eye, choose *not* to see. The notion of spirituality addresses forces which cannot be 'seen', and yet which play a significant determining role in our lives, and indeed may play a crucial part in what it means to *be* alive. Returning to Freud, he claimed as one of his supreme achievements the insight that our emotional life is ruled not by a monarchical self but by unconscious forces to which the fragile ego is subject. Like gravity and energy, the unconscious is not directly detectable by the senses, but made 'visible' by its effects in our actions, dreams, and life experience.

In a related, yet distinct way, the term spirituality captures the *emergent patterns of meaning and connectedness* which shape our beliefs, behaviour, and relationships. If the unconscious encapsulates the 'unthought known' (Bollas, 2019), spirituality points to the 'known unthought', in the sense that the term affirms that there are dimensions to life which resist representation or description, yet which shape what really matters to us.

Secularity

Secular, our next problematic word, literally means 'in time' or 'in an age'. Its non-religious use—such as 'secular' oak trees—refers to natural phenomena that are cyclical or recurring. In a spiritual or religious context, secularism is contrasted with the timelessness of eternity, and a transcendent deity. The outstanding contemporary scholar of the secular is Charles Taylor (2007). He differentiates three meanings of the term. The frst, as used in mediaeval times, distinguished occupations that were secular, that is, trades, from those that were ecclesiastical such as the priesthood. Taylor's second sense of secular goes hand-in-hand with the Enlightenment, when non-religious spaces, physical and conceptual, such as parliaments, schools, scientific organisations, non-biblical texts, and—relevant to our discussion—hospitals and health practitioners, began to emerge and rival ecclesiastical hegemony.

A Secular Age, the title of Taylor's magisterial book, refers to the third and modern sense of secular. Even for the religious, belief in God can now no longer be taken for granted and unproblematic, and is willy-nilly nested in a world of disenchantment, whether partial or total. To the extent that the non-secular remains vital and valid, it encompasses a multiplicity of faiths and non-faiths, beliefs and un-beliefs, and their accompanying practices. Many people in Western Christian or post-Christian societies describe themselves as 'spiritual but not religious'. Without specific adherence to a belief system, or regularly attending Church, they might, for instance, hold to the idea of a 'higher power' (as in Alcoholics Anonymous, see Vaillant, 2009), agree with Pascal that the heart has its reasons of which the head knows nothing, and/or with Hamlet that there are more things in heaven and earth than are dreamt of in his mundane friend Horatio's philosophy.

Taylor contends that this modernistic pluralism contributes to a sense of unease in both believers and non-believers. The former feel the need to *defend* their faith. The rise of fundamentalism is one manifestation of this, since more liberal versions of religion tend to merge imperceptibly into secularism. For non-believers, which probably includes the majority of psychotherapists, exclusive secularisation sets up a sense of something missing, a yearning for what Taylor calls '*fullness*', related to fulfilment, the need to find a dimension beyond the everyday parameters of contemporary life (cf. Resnick, 2023).

This third sense then is the one most relevant to psychotherapy. Whatever their 'psychopathology', people—and their therapists—are drawn to the challenges of psychotherapy because it seems to offer, usually implicitly, a chance to redress feelings of emptiness and anomie, to go beyond the two-dimensionality of modern life. The reverberations of psychoanalysis suggest the possibility of deep relationships of psychic intimacy and interchange—with oneself and others—in contrast to relational superficiality, perversity, or its non-existence. For Freud the militant atheist, the essence of psychoanalysis was to help people live *without* the 'illusory' comforts of religion; to foster the ironic courage of a humanistic existence in which, in the context of analytic relationship, the totality of psychic life, good and evil, could be faced and endured.

This anti-spirituality spirit certainly lives on in some psychoanalytic quarters. A distant root of this book was the author's shock when, as a psychotherapeutic newcomer, he heard a senior member of the profession publicly pronounce that a belief in God was incompatible with being a psychoanalyst. The shock was not because I took theological offence, but rather that a crucial feature of the psychoanalysis to which I aspired was its valuation of ambiguity, non-knowing, and all-embracing acceptance of whatever patients (and by implication) their therapists brought into the relationship. The idea that there was a no-go anti-theistic boundary seemed fundamentally at variance with this ambiance of openness.

Within the context of the session, the ultimate non-judgemental ethic prevails: 'I am human, I consider nothing that is human alien to me' (Terence: 'Homo sum, humani nihil a me alienum puto'). Therapists, albeit in a very different way, learn as much from their patients as vice versa. A personal aim in this project was, as a secular psychotherapist, the hope that I might learn from those who had sought religious rather than psychotherapeutic pathways towards Taylorian fullness.

Religion

A number of other terms need definition in order to orient the discussion, where no doubt my theological amateurism will further reveal itself. The first is *religion* itself. The etymology of the term is debated. Alternative theories turn on the vowel *i* or *e*, both of which are relevant to this project. One view is that it comes from the Latin *legare*, to read, and *re*-ligion implies ritual *re*-reading of sacred texts, a practice typical of orthodox Judaism, Islam, and Hinduism. This is the sense that Freud (1907b) seized on in his tendentious comparison between obsessional compulsive disorder (OCD) and religion, seeing both as 'meaningless' behavioural repetitions designed to stave off danger. Strangely, although he saw therapy's task as finding the hidden meaning in an obsessional ritual, he failed to see that religious ritual also contained meaning and spoke to the inner worlds of worshippers—at the very least to impose order on a morally chaotic universe—just as OCD rituals offer short-term comfort to their sufferers. One might see OCD as a doomed-to-failure attempt to minimise free energy by eliminating uncertainty and the vagaries of fate. Nor, perhaps, was Freud fully in touch with his own obsessionality, and the ways in which it shaped his invention of the comparable rituals of psychoanalysis, whose influence still prevails today.

The second sense, emphasised by St Augustine, whose thinking lies behind much of modern theology, comes from *ligare*, to bind, and refers to the *community* of religion, the web of connections—formal and informal—between its adherents, which characterise religious practice. This assumes increasing importance in our atomised modern world in which neo-liberal celebration of autonomy and individual freedom comes at the price of a lack of connection and group living. I shall argue that binding of 'free energy' by the combined efforts of therapist and patient lie at the heart of the psychotherapeutic enterprise, and can therefore, in this limited sense at least, be deemed relatedly 'spiritual'.

Faith

Our next term is *faith*, which derives from the Latin *fides*, meaning trust or confidence. The role of trust and faith forms an important bridge between the worlds of spirituality and psychoanalysis. In Taylor's secular contemporary world, religious belief entails a 'leap of faith' from the evidential ground of everyday experience into the unknown unknown, yet which, aware of our limitations, while sensing the unlimitedness of the universe, we 'know' to be there. Likewise, for Bion (1970) faith in the psychoanalytic context affirms the presence of an unknowable reality, 'O', as in his quasi-mathematically schema he liked to call it. 'O' corresponds roughly to Kantian 'noumenon'—that which has not yet been, in Bion's terms, 'metabolised' with the help of the mother/analyst or religious faith-leap, and is therefore inaccessible for mental representation. One can hear an echo of the Buddhist primal maternal sound, Ohm, in Bion's O-invocation.

Militant atheism and analytic philosophy (Ayer, 2000; Dawkins, 2008; Hitchens, 2007) contrast evidence-based *knowledge* with what they see as delusional *belief*, thereby dismissing the entirety of spirituality and religion as unwarranted speculation. As the mathematician Laplace is said to have replied to Napoleon when asked where God fitted into his schema: 'I have no need of that hypothesis.' Critics of psychoanalysis have taken a similar line, arguing—often tendentiously—that the evidence for many of its central tenets, for example, oedipal theory, infantile sexuality, and the death instinct, are at best questionable, at worst shibboleths inaccessible to Popperian refutation. Again, during my psychiatric infancy, a difficult moment occurred when, on learning that I was psychotherapeutically inclined, a senior colleague raised his eyebrows, exclaiming dismissively, 'Oh, I *see*, you're a *believer!*'

In fact, both attachment theory and contemporary neuroscience now provide strong evidential support for the view that much of human adaptation and its associated cognition, including analytic philosophy, is based on faith and trust (cf. Eagleton, 2009). Living organisms, ourselves included, survive, thrive, and reproduce in environments beset with uncertainty and danger. As I argued in the previous chapter, our Bayesian brains make ever-changing, and continuously revised statistical *predictions* about the present and future likely state of the world, drawing on and extrapolating from prior experience and available evidence (Holmes, 2020). In that sense, faith is an essential and integral part of living, while psychological illness is dogged by faith-failures—clinging to the past, feeling unable to find pathways to the future, shutting out reality and retreating into unmodified realms of top-down-ness.

A related notion is that of 'epistemic trust' (Fonagy & Allison, 2014) which links secure attachment with the necessary faith children must ascribe to worldviews transmitted to them, first by their parents, primary caregivers, and later by teachers, mentors, friends, and the wider informational world. Epistemic trust is far from confined to our species, or even to mammals. Social animals generally closely observe and mimic the behaviour of their conspecifics, learning from them which environments are likely to be safe, food-rich, to be avoided, etc. (Laland, 2017). In rapidly changing environmental conditions working things out for oneself may be a necessary fallback strategy. But in general, relying on cultural transmission via epistemic trust for the overall parameters of existence is more efficient. This creates less disruptive free energy residue, is therefore energetically advantageous, and so favoured by natural selection. We don't need to reinvent the wheel before setting off for work on our bicycles every morning.

Epistemic trust—its necessity, benefits, and pathologies—is an issue for both religion and psychoanalysis. Learning whom and what to trust is an outcome which psychotherapy implicitly aims to foster, *in vitro* in the analytic session, later *in vivo* generalising to emotionally pedagogic relationships in the wider world. Attachment research shows that securely attached children are able to discern when to rely on their teachers and when to think for themselves, while the insecurely attached tend either to be excessively self-reliant/avoidant, or overdependent/preoccupied (Holmes & Slade, 2017).

Several of the interviewees to be described later had experienced a crisis in the faith within which they had been brought up. They could no longer trust the precepts and priests whose formulae were so much at variance with their lived experience. One woman, despite being both abused and neglected by her arranged-marriage husband, was told by her parents and her orthodox rabbi that it was her wifely duty to stay with him for the sake of the family and her children. Only when she transposed her epistemic trust system to a therapist, who emphasised and reinforced her own *self*-trust that her marriage was emotionally damaging, did she regain her sense of agency and begin to recover from depression and concomitant suicidal feelings.

Sacred

Another related theme is the notion of the *sacred*. Sacred derives from the Latin *sacer*, dedicated to a God, or consecrated. The term, which overlaps with *holy*, is used mainly in relation to objects or places, differentiating them from the profane or mundane world of everyday affairs.

A church and its venerated objects—vessels, icons, etc.—is a sacred place where the normal rules of society do not apply. In times of war non-participants often congregate in churches, and bombing or setting fire to such places is considered a particularly egregious war crime. During communist rule in Eastern Europe, churches were one of the few places where people felt free to express their true views, and even totalitarian rule tended to leave them alone (an exception is the persecuted Falun Gong movement in present-day China). My very limited experience of mullah-dominated Iran is that psychotherapy trainings and seminars are somewhat protected from Islamic fundamentalism, where free discussion and even relaxation of dress codes for women can be subtly unveiled.

I shall argue that the psychotherapeutic consulting room can similarly be considered a sacred space, and that there is a valid secular version of the sacred. This is well described by Malik (2023) in his comparison of Vermeer's luminous paintings of 'interiors'—his subjects reading letters, pouring milk, flirting while playing at the virginals— with the novelist Marilynne Robinson:

> There is a scene in Marilynne Robinson's novel *Gilead* in which the main character, John Ames, a pastor, walking to his church, comes across a young couple in the street. 'The sun had come up brilliantly after a heavy rain, and the trees were glistening and very wet,' he recalls. The young man ahead of him 'jumped up and caught hold of a branch, and a storm of luminous water came pouring down on the two of them, and they laughed and took off running, the girl sweeping water off her hair and her dress'. It was 'a beautiful thing to see, like something from a myth'. In such moments, 'it is easy to believe … that water was made primarily for blessing, and only secondarily for growing vegetables or doing the wash.
>
> It is a wonderful, luminous passage, typical of Robinson's ability to discover the lyrical even within the mundane. Deeply Christian, and Calvinist, there is in her writing a spiritual force that springs from her faith. She would probably describe that scene as the discovery of a divine presence in the world. And yet, flowing out of that scene, is also an awareness that transcends

the religious. It is the uncovering of something very human, a celebration of our ability to find the poetic in our simplest activities. (Malik, 2023)

Transcendence vs immanence

The final definitional theme is the contrast between the terms *transcendent* and *immanent*. Much sophisticated theological philosophy centres upon this issue. My simplified understanding is that transcendence and immanence encompass either dualistic or monistic worldviews. A transcendent model—typical of Abrahamic religions—makes a clear distinction between the world of God and the spirit on the one hand, and the material world which we mortals occupy on the other, although the former is partially accessible through prayer and mystical experience, and is entered into in the putative afterlife. Immanence—typical of Buddhism and panentheism but also in the heretical Judaism of Spinoza—is non-dualistic, does not bracket off the holy from the mundane, and if monotheistic, posits an omnipotent deity who makes his/her presence manifest in the material world. For Spinoza, God is co-extensive with the world as we experience it, and we humans are mere forms of that materiality—waves in a panentheist ocean (Pargament, 2013), a metaphor also much used in Buddhism, and interestingly, also in contemporary quantum-based physics (Rovelli, 2022).

There are echoes of the immanent in the ambiance of psychoanalytic psychotherapy too, which, its proponents like Eigen (1998) and Bion (1990) suggest, at times can generate mystical egoless states in which the self is merged with the encompassing world. By contrast, in the 'Zurich' Jungian worldview, the 'collective unconscious' has a transcendent quality arising out of our psychobiological heritage which erupts from 'elsewhere' into the individual life in the form of dreams, creativity, and unwilled actions. I shall be arguing in my conclusion that an ecologically oriented twenty-first-century psychotherapy has the capacity to point beyond this historically contextualised (cf. Hickel, 2021) immanence–transcendence split.

CHAPTER 4

The place of psychotherapy in contemporary culture

My argument thus far is that there is a vacant and significant space in our private and public discourse, which contemporary psychoanalytic psychotherapy can and should occupy. But to make such a large claim for such a semi-marginalised discipline as psychoanalysis is inherently problematic. The role, theory, and practice of psychoanalytic psychotherapy are all 'difficult', in ways that are creative, but sometimes impenetrable to the uninitiated. Psychoanalytic ideas are hard to understand and operationalise; they eschew simple solutions to complex problems, and, with their emphasis on the negative or 'shadow' sides of life, are morally disquieting. At its most radical, psychoanalysis occupies a space largely outside the 'Overton window'—that is, ideas that are admissible in everyday political, social, and scientific discourse. Taken seriously, psychoanalysis calls into question the prevailing hegemony of late-capitalist, commodified, individualistic, utilitarian viewpoints—a challenge which, ironically, often goes unnoticed and unheralded by practitioners themselves.

For Freud, the invention of psychoanalysis overturned the supremacy of the overweening ego, replacing it as a psychic force with the mysterious and evolution-forged unconscious. This perspective applies at a social as well as an individual level. I'm suggesting that psychoanalytic psychotherapy has much in common with cultural formations traditionally located in organised religion. Alongside its proven efficacy as a psychological treatment, psychoanalytic culture abuts people's yearning for spiritual as well as material sustenance.

Let's start with a fly-on-the-wall's-eye view of the therapeutic process in action. A suffering person sits with a listener-witness in a room. There is talk, now silence—or the reverse. Feelings are the focus. Tears appear. Patterns, elaborated into stories, emerge. These are shaped, questioned, modified. Expectations are confounded. The therapist is a real person—and a figment of the client's inner world. Superfluidity abounds. Nothing is complete, there is always more to come. Framing this uncertainty, the encounter zone of therapy-participants is defined and bounded: a space that is warm, comfortable, confidential, and free from interruptions. Time is walled off, a temporal wedge in which, for fifty minutes, give or take, the routines and chaotic impingements of normal life are held at bay.

In this chapter I outline three levels at which this psychoanalytic space–time operates: the inner world of individuals and groups; the actual spaces of therapy sessions themselves; and the metaphorical place/space of psychoanalysis as a cultural phenomenon. I start with the second of these, since, unlike the other two, what 'happens' in therapy sessions, externally at least, can be observed, recorded, and analysed without the theoretical preconceptions and prejudices that go with the first and third of these constructs.

What happens in a psychotherapy session?

Therapy as praxis

A place of worship is a predefined space—church, mosque, synagogue, shrine, etc.—which the supplicant enters, voluntarily or ritually, and where expected behaviours are displayed, while others are prohibited. Adherents kneel, genuflect, prostrate themselves, sup, sip, sing, read, pray, intone, and move their limbs in ways learned through observing, following, studying, and routinising—typically from childhood onward. Sex and violence are outlawed, although exhortations to both, explicit or implicit, are common, alongside invocations of the attachment triad of altruism, caring, and pity. This, in Aristotle's term, is religious *praxis*—what actually is done and said in church space—as opposed to beliefs, cosmologies, and controversies.

Rustin (2019) and Barratt (2012), in different ways, have applied the Aristotelian notion of praxis to psychotherapy. For Rustin, Freud's invention of the therapy room, comprising a prone patient alongside the interpreting analyst, was a technological innovation comparable to the inventions of lens grinders of fifteenth-century Venice, whose methods enabled Galileo to initiate the heliocentric revolution. There were of course forms of what we would now call psychotherapy that predate psychoanalysis. But Freud moved therapy beyond a 'doing to' form of 'placebology'—hypnotherapy, electrotherapy, etc.—to 'being with', carving out a new science of hitherto unmapped relational experience. This was, and is, unconscious mental life as revealed in dreams, fantasies, and free associations, therapeutically gathered up into meaningful patterns by the analyst, and, in Bion's term, 'metabolised' in the transitional space of the analyst–patient dyad.

For Barratt, psychoanalytic praxis refers to the actual *experience* of therapy, whether as patient or analyst (the former being a precondition for working as the latter). In a Wittgensteinian way, therapy, like speech, musicianship, sports, or game playing, can only be learned through doing—in other words, praxis. By experiencing consulting room confusion, terror, rage, lostness, and despair—alongside hope, love, and sensitive acceptance—one comes to understand life's value and meaning, and, in equal measure, its failures and limitations.

This predicates the epistemological dilemma confronting psychoanalytic psychotherapy. During an informal discussion about the evidence-base for psychoanalysis, a colleague pronounced, 'Well, I just know from personal experience that psychoanalysis *works*.' How does one differentiate this assertion from a religious believer who might say, 'I just know that God exists. I hear him [*sic*] speak to me every day'? Both are 'right', but not perhaps in the ways that the speakers might suppose. In the terms of the previous chapter, both are making spiritual if not scientific sense. There is convincing evidence that religious practice has beneficial effects on physical and mental health. Similarly, psychotherapy meets robust criteria for effectiveness and efficacy.

However, the objective 'mechanisms' by which religion and psychotherapy 'work' may flow from factors unknown to their practitioners. The narratives with which believers imbue their beliefs are in themselves comforting, and may underpin their overall efficacy—belief leading to trust, leading to hope, leading to psychological health—but bear no necessary causal relationship to the benefits they bring. From an FEM perspective, beliefs are sets of top-down precepts, parables and epigrams which bind free energy as best they can, but, spiritually speaking, there is always a quantum left unaccounted for. The truth or otherwise of beliefs is left to be metabolised in the transitional zone of interpersonal relatedness.

Agency

As touched on in the introduction, a key aspect of praxis in the psychotherapy setting is helping clients to develop a sense of *agency*. Agency implies being an active participant in one's own world, able to influence—for good or ill—one's fellow humans and therefore, to an extent at least, shape one's own emotions and destiny. Many of those who seek psychotherapy feel, and objectively are, disempowered. Abuse, multiple traumata, cumulative adverse childhood experiences, neglectful or intrusive parenting, social deprivation, and bullying—all strangle agency in its cradle. Feelings of helplessness, hopelessness, and resigned passivity prevail. A life of victimhood beckons with its 'secondary gain' attractions. Sufferers' narratives are dominated by justified accounts of blame and resentment, which—for the sake of immediate psychological survival—are then often repeatedly deployed, but to their long-term disadvantage. It can be discomfiting, but ultimately liberating for clients to be gently reminded that they have at some level 'chosen' to inactivate their agency, and that other options were, and remain, open.

Clients seeking therapy can be thought of as 'dis-spirited'. The play space of spiritual life between the inner world and external reality has collapsed. The vicissitudes of material and emotional deprivation press up against the subjects' suffering with no hope of escape. Defensive manoeuvres, at the price of sacrificing spirituality, close down transitional space—the locus where psychic pain can be first felt, named, objectified, and, partially at least, transcended.

A prime aim of psychotherapy is to highlight and then to begin to reverse this passivity and so to restore or instate a sense of agency. This—at a number of levels—can also be seen as a validation of spiritual life. The simple fact of seeking out and attending therapy is an agentic step. The benefit implicit in the very act of 'doing something' about one's problems should not be underestimated, especially in contrast to submitting oneself passively or involuntarily to a protocolised system characterised by blunderbuss medication, banal agony-aunt type advice, or, in extreme cases enforced 'treatment'. There would be a parallel here with the more overtly 'spiritual' decision to attend a church service or join a religious group.

A second, agency-enhancing factor lies in the fact that the psychotherapy client finds herself taken seriously and listened to, which may often be an entirely novel experience. The transitional space of therapy is a spiritual restorative. In psychoanalytic psychotherapy, the client is always the initiator, however unaccustomed and even resistant she may be to this role. Gergely and Watson (1996) studied baby and mother facial interactions in the first few months of life. They noted that key features of the mother's side of this non-verbal dialogue were what they termed *contingency* and *marking*. The mother contingently waits for the infant to make the first move in their 'conversation', and then responds with a marked reflection of the child's mood or state of mind. This simple procedure can be thought of as instilling even in early life a child's sense of self-awareness, autonomy, and proto-individuation. These everyday yet vital interactions lay the foundations for secure attachment and epistemic trust in the sense of being heard and held in mind. In the second half of the first year these 'conversations' become yet more playful, jazzy, and innovative, further enhancing the child's sense of agency and autonomy and creativity.

Analogously, psychoanalytic psychotherapy creates an ambiance in which the therapist holds back, especially at the start of sessions, playing the part of the expectant caregiver, waiting for the client to get the therapeutic ball rolling, ready to underline and validate the patient's authentic affective verbal and non-verbal gestures.

James, a gifted amateur painter, sought therapy, ostensibly because he found himself torn between staying in a bureaucratic job which he found dull, but which offered him a degree of security, or branching out his own as an artist, with all the anxiety that accompanies a sense of excitement and creativity. His dilemma had resonances in his developmental history. His lone-parent mother had had a serious illness when he was four years old and he had, in his words, been 'dumped' with child-averse grandparents for several months. His ongoing dilemma was the divide between playfulness and fear on the one hand, or a degree of safety but stifled creativity on the other.

Initially James assumed that his therapist would tell him what to do—whether to 'dump' his job and playfully paint, or stay safe but emotionally numb. He discovered instead that the therapist was interested in his free associations and dreams, and—to his horror—asserted that he and his unconscious knew more about himself than anyone else could. He was, as the therapist put it, the 'world-expert on himself', if only he could allow himself to be so.

The prime driver for agency, a sense of being able to make choices and bring them into effect, is affect. Feelings are the driver behind the wish to achieve a degree of happiness/contentment or freedom from mental pain, even if that process may entail temporary augmentation of that pain, tolerable if accompanied by a co-regulating other on that journey. Agency, and accompanying affect are scary. At first patients need the therapist at hand to make sure their choices don't lead them into an abyss. Action is the tangible end result of feelings, wishes, and desires. Therapy is an empowering passivity antidote because it brings this triad into the light. They come to a surface that is unique to their possessors. At the same time they are helped to observe the process in action. This might be expressed existentially—and possibly somewhat pompously—as follows:

These are my feelings that I have hitherto ignored, suppressed, avoided, or attributed to others. Now I can see them for what they are and also identify where they belong—in myself. I am an *agent*, in whom sensation, affect, and action are inextricably and linearly linked. I am the author of my own life, with all its confusions, miseries, and setbacks, alongside what fragments of happiness and creativity I have also managed to achieve. Through therapy I have reclaimed my agency, but also become aware, as I tell my story, of the ways in which I have been brutally robbed of agency, or circumstances have conspired to limit its thriving. But I can no longer avoid taking responsibility for the choices, conscious or unconscious, I have made, and the ways in which I contributed to my own unhappiness and the unhappiness of others. I also acknowledge the counterpart to agency is the contingency of life and the randomness of the circumstances—my socio-historical destiny—into which I have been thrown. That in turn leads me to try to forgive those who have failed to provide the care and trust I needed, recognising that they too were carrying the weight of their own parental and social failures into the next generation. That in turn prompts me to work towards first acknowledging, but then forgiving myself for the neglect, cruelty, and blame I have inflicted on others.

In relation to agency, two more aspects are important. Because the therapist maintains an ambiguous and reticent participant–observer position, the client–therapist interaction is a microcosm of the clients' relational signature. Transferentially, clients will enact long-established entrenched patterns of being with self and others. The benignly neutral therapist is then in a position to suggest to clients how they have shaped and continue to shape these interactions so as to maintain familiarity, avoid mental pain, and minimise surprise. Many therapists' comments and interpretations are in the service of fostering agency, taking the client away from the externals of their life and back to their own mental universe and the part they play in bringing it into being, but also how, in 'we-mode' transitional space, 'alone in the presence of the other', new and more complex patterns can be forged.

This sense of ownership of oneself has a spiritual aspect in that it entails acknowledgement of those aspects of one's history and inner world that are beyond the ego's purview.

A therapist might question:
'I wonder what your unconscious was up to when it guided you to marry X?'

'Well maybe I just wanted to feel normal. Everyone else I knew was getting married ... and X agreed with me that marriage is only a bit of paper ...'

'So, given your rather bleak childhood, maybe there was something about that ambivalence and denial of intimacy that drew you to X ... you could be close and distant at the same time, a token marriage that somehow failed to get off the page.'

Therapeutic *poesis*

For Aristotle, praxis was one leg of a triad which also included *theoria* (pure thought), and creativity and innovative action, which he termed *poesis*. Therapy can also be seen as a species of *poesis*, since the kinds of conversations which go on in consulting rooms tend to be unique to that setting. Psychoanalytic psychotherapy can be thought of as 'talking to oneself out loud'. Therapists are privy to these internal conversations that may never reach ears outside the consulting room, even with the subject's nearest and dearest, figures who are in any case often sadly conspicuous by their absence in client's lives. For client and therapist both, a therapy session can be thought of as a form of everyday art, characterised by making a mess (and clearing up afterwards!), no-holds-barred speech, and following where one's creative impulses lead. Meanwhile, the mundane realities of the client's and therapist's lives are temporarily left at the consulting room door, allowing a unique and novel thought or dream to be forged within the allocated space-time of their encounter.

In this process all but the most austerely pristine psychotherapeutic conversations probably include 'non-analytic' elements. Advice-giving, sympathy, and humour are in the therapeutic mix, as an intimate-partner *idiolect* (Lear, 2011) is built up between client and therapist. Honesty and the self-revelation implicit in free association remain psychoanalytic psychotherapy's hallmarks. Not unlike the role of prayer in religion, they nest at its spiritual core.

If therapy is to make a difference, these innovative relational conversations will ultimately have to be translated into changes and choices in the externals of the client's life. New ways will be found of managing emotions, especially anxiety and depression, or, if psychotic, the symptoms of mental illness, together with changed patterns of relationship, friendship, occupation, and group affiliations. These re-figurations of external space spring from psychotherapy's capacity to bring about a changed geometry of the inner, and, in the terms of this discussion, spiritual world.

Psychotherapy and the inner world

When I was training as a psychiatrist we had a teaching session with a prominent psychoanalyst and family therapist. He opened his session by bouncing into the classroom and drawing on the blackboard a child's version of a chocolate box house: roof, chimney, two windows, a front door with a flower-bedecked garden path leading up to it. 'What's that?' he asked. Nonplussed, 'a house', we dutifully replied. To this he countered, 'Well, *I've* never seen a real house like that.' He went on to suggest that his depicted 'house' was in reality a representation of the *self*: an inner space of privacy and where emotional and bodily needs are manifest—caring, loving, hating, feeding, bathing, nakedness, excretion, sex—walled off by a boundary whose exterior presents a smiling face to the world, and whose architectural or 'linguistic' vernacular conforms, more or less, to that of its immediate neighbours.

For Winnicott and his successors (e.g. Bollas, 2019) therapy takes place in a transition zone between inner and outer, a play space where fantasy and reality overlap and where damaged infantile omnipotence— with its accompanying deficits in agency—can begin to rebuild, and clients start to rehearse the lineaments of a life of their own.

The inner world can be thought of as a space within the self, a place where sensations/feelings arise and reside, encompassing both mind and body, a locus where thoughts originate, where dreams come into being, the nidus of identity. This inner world is essentially private, inaccessible to external scrutiny or scientific examination and numeration, throwing up the ultimate 'hard problem' of consciousness (Solms, 2021). If we rephrase Descartes's famous phrase as 'I *feel* therefore I am', affect lies at the heart of this inner world. Our capacity to feel emotions is the guarantee of our existence and an existential/spiritual bedrock. This me-ness is co-extensive with the way we experience the redness of red (Humphrey, 2023), the bitterness of acid, the passion and tenderness of love, the tearfulness of loss, and the hatefulness of hatred. Bateman (2022) tracks the progress of therapy from 'I-mode' (a kind of infantile self-centredness), through 'me-mode' where the client thus begins to feel and objectify her affective life, to 'we-mode' where new realities can be co-constructed from mutual 'me-modes'.

The Janus-faced inner world

From a psychodynamic perspective, the paradox of the inner world is that it is simultaneously intensely relational, and inescapably private and individual. Although the umbilical cord is severed, the newborn baby remains physiologically linked to the caregiver via holding, feeding, soothing, rocking, etc., underpinned by their accompanying endocrinological infrastructure (especially oxytocin, Feldman, 2015). The baby's nervous system is linked to her mother's brain no less than were their circulations in utero. Relational neuroscience postulates an invisible mental placenta as vital to survival as palpable body parts. There is intense right brain-to-right brain connectivity as mothers interact with their babies (Schore, 2001) or continuous projective processes in which baby and mother's feelings pass to-and-fro, via sight, sound, and touch in empathic resonance, one with another (Stern, 1985).

This set-up, while in the widest sense dialogic, is also and obviously asymmetric. The caregiver's task is to help bring the baby's inner world into being, keeping her own inner world demarcated, albeit semi-permeably, from that of the child. The caregiver provides external 'scaffolding' as the baby learns to point, join, insist, walk, talk, etc. The mother's accurate empathy and reflection, via contingency and marked mirroring, helps the securely attached child to identify, own, and make use of her own thoughts and feelings. These processes are compromised in the various forms of insecure attachment (Holmes & Slade, 2017).

By the age of three, this child–caregiver dialogue will have changed in two Janus-faced ways. Outwardly, communication is no longer purely gestural, but mediated by the bootstrapped miracle of language ('well done', 'clever girl', 'no, that's not good', etc.). Language places the child squarely in the universe of shared brains. Going in the opposite direction, conversation is now internalised, so children begin to talk with themselves. At this three-year-old stage self-talk is often accessible to an external observer, who can eavesdrop as the child plays 'alone in the presence of the mother' (Meares, 2016; Winnicott, 1992). By the age of five this self-conversation becomes increasingly silent and private. By adulthood, an internal I–Thou conversation is fully established, even if, as in avoidant attachment, the self is sometime deaf to itself. Swimming through the imperceptible time-stream of days, the mind, consciously and/or unconsciously, explicitly and/or implicitly, asks itself what it is feeling, thinking, hoping, and planning, and adjusts perceptions and actions in the light of these.

One can direct this internal attention to the past ('I was a bit of an idiot in those days, I drank far too much'), present ('right now I'm just longing for a drink'), or future ('from now on I plan to attend AA meetings much more regularly'). One of the tasks and technologies of psychoanalytic psychotherapy, especially free association, is to capture and once more to externalise this internal talk so that, with the help of the therapist, it can be examined and modified in the direction of greater self-understanding and self-acceptance.

The essence of this model is the dialectic between the privacy of the inner world and the projective interplay—'duets for one'—between the inner worlds of intimates, parents and children, lovers, and, for the purposes of this discussion, therapists and their clients.

An evolutionary perspective: the Markov blanket

Here evolution has set itself a problem. In order to be biologically viable, cells, organisms, or groups are needs-be isolated one from another. As with the wall of our teacher's self-house, their very individuality depends on their boundedness. A drop of ink in a glass of water will quickly disperse and diffuse, while a single celled organism of the same size and shape will, while it lives, maintain its structure (Friston, 2010). But in order to survive, an organism also needs to gather not just material nutrients across the cell boundary and to excrete waste, but also to acquire and assimilate *information* about its surrounding context: salinity, pH, food gradients, friends or foes, etc. Alongside its physiological role as a self-world boundary, the cell wall is also a two-way information channel, or 'Markov blanket' (Kirchhoff et al., 2017).

The Markov blanket is a statistical concept that defines this informational boundary of systems, including our brains. Our knowledge of the 'external' world, which includes parts of the body external to the brain, is constrained by the statistical information provided by the senses. The world is light-flooded; inside our skull darkness reigns. There is a built-in limit or 'blanket' between the knowledge afforded to our embodied self and William James's (2002) 'buzzing booming' world of external reality. In order to create a coherent picture of the world and adaptively guide interaction with it, the brain draws on its Bayes-derived top-down store of models of this external reality and—moment to moment—aligns these with incoming sensations in a predictive way.

For instance … 'Let's assume, given its size and configuration, and this suburban context, that that black feline I see on the horizon is a cat not a panther. Oh, but I did read that one had escaped from the zoo recently, so better be careful, and take a closer look.' If there is more than one such organism in a niche, their adaptation and survival will be enhanced by concerted action and information transfer—hormonal, electrochemical, auditory, visual, etc. 'I think I'll ask my companion what he/she thinks that black blob might be'. Ultimately two such 'individuals' may 'decide' to amalgamate—by incorporation as in the case of mitochondria, or into multicellular organisms, and beyond them, as in the case of our primate ancestors, into families, groups, and societies. This multicellularity, or group membership, facilitates specialisation and differentiation. Thus the self-group dialectic reaches deep into our psychobiological heritage—an individual can only survive by being part of a whole, and yet if subsumed into that whole ceases to exist as an individual.

During this process of interpersonalising, the uniqueness of the inner world is largely hidden—a secret ballot in the democracy of group action. Privacy brings a number of advantages. It mitigates against 'groupthink'—one of the key issues in evolution is the unpredictability of environments and the range of phenotypes needed to maximise adaptation. Difference matters and conveys several advantages. Having available a variety of responses helps group survival. This lies at the root of the evolution of sex which ensures variation in contrast to the otherwise more economically efficient asexual reproduction. Similarly, in extreme danger or adversity, group-avoidant attachment may be more adaptive than secure varieties—during a fire in a theatre an avoidant individual may be more likely to survive, breaking windows to save their own skin, and showing the way for the more securely attached. An inner world protected by a Markov blanket is a bulwark against relational trauma brought about by dysfunctional upbringing, exploitation, and/or abuse. Uncertainty about another's feelings and intentions leads to appropriate cautiousness and hyper-vigilance about friend/foe differentiation. As a virtual space, the inner world enables the individual to carry out 'thought experiments'; in other words to consider a range of options, appraisals, and possibilities prior to, and clearly differentiated from action.

The Markov blanket concept articulates the inescapable 'veil of ignorance' (Rawls, 2001) between ourselves and the world. Our perceptions are necessarily perspectival, limited by our physiology and our prior experience. We are constantly making guesses about 'what is going on out there'. Faith and belief represent attempts to derive coherence and meaning from the limited and constrained information our senses provide. Here God, the ultimate explanandum, can be our final resort, especially when, in a 'multicellular' way, the deity is shared with others.

> When I was training as a psychiatrist one of my very first patients was a man who in a depressive and psychotic state had thrown himself off a high suspension bridge—and survived. For him this was incontrovertible proof that God existed and was his saviour. On recovery, he changed his name from John Smith to 'Redemptionist Israel' and joined a fundamentalist church. He continued to experience a number of psychotic delusions. My professor encouraged me to approach the church and to attend one of the services with my patient (such things were possible in those less pressurised and more thoughtful days of medical training), which I duly did. I found that the church elders were hugely caring and loving towards Redemptionist, but were clearly able to differentiate his unique psychotic belief system from their shared religious outlook.

Transitionality in psychotherapy and religion

Comparing the psychotherapeutic with the spiritual outlook on uncertainty, one can see that psychotherapy too tries to tap into the highest level of the top-down hierarchy. But rather than offering a global uncertainty-reducing precept such as God or divine-dictated scripture, psychotherapy relies on examining the state of uncertainty itself. In this mostly benign division of the self—the self reflecting on the self—a second perspective or voice is required. The therapist's role is to bring to light and then question the fundamental assumptions which determine a person's relational world. These are often deeply ingrained and resistant to evidential challenge.

> 'Deep down I just *know* that I'm unlovable.'
> 'Older siblings-figures will *always* be preferred over me.'
> 'The world is irremediably unsafe, there's *no one* I can really turn to for comfort.'

(Note the 'marking' or italicisation with which a therapist might reflect back these assertions, thereby implicitly questioning them.)

As in Redemptionist's case, for the religious, such assumptions can be trumped by a God who loves, favours, and protects. But there will still always be questions. How can I be *sure* of my convictions? Does he/she *really* love me? Rather than combatting uncertainty with faith, psychotherapy takes off from it, replacing defensive certainties with embraced states of unknowing, self-scientific questioning of assumptions. It will juxtapose maladaptive anachronistic relational models with more complex ones. This is done in an atmosphere of affective arousal induced by the intensity of the psychotherapeutic attention which in turn makes psychic restructuring more likely.

Although the spiritual and the psychotherapeutic diverge in their solutions, both are struggling with the same problem of uncertainty, and for both an intermediary is needed together with a sequestered arena: priest, guru, or therapist, in church, temple, or consulting room. The battle to relinquish cherished but maladaptive assumptions with more consensually valid ones is played out in these sacred spaces.

In contemporary life the inner world where this battle might take place has become increasingly etiolated or discounted. Fluidity, creativity, and provisionality of thought and representation are replaced with the concrete, the superficial (in the literal sense), and the fixed. Life is lived on the surface. Identity has replaced process, the potentiality of development discarded for the illusions of the pseudo-definite. In a neo-liberal environment the self and its accoutrements—habits, dress, diet, appearance, hobbies—are targeted as potential commodities, in accordance with the dictates of a capitalistic culture. Thus does capitalism invade the self, bringing all to the surface. Even on the Left, skin colour in itself is seen as a determinant of life chances—the 'look like me' factor—rather than historical processes of enslavement, exploitation, and prejudice that speak to colonised inner worlds rather than merely that which is visible.

As antidote to this imperceptible and insidious process, psychoanalysis provides through the therapeutic relationship both a language and a praxis where the inner world can begin to be reinstated. So too does the world of non-dogmatic spirituality. For Buddhists, overcoming suffering entails the realisation that inner and outer worlds are in states of constant flux, and the necessity therefore to embrace rather than resist change and transience. Where there is movement there is hope.

> Sean, aged seventeen, was witness to an appalling trauma, when his father, encountering his mother embracing another man, shot her dead before his very eyes. The father was given to a long prison sentence, thereby subjecting Sean to double orphanhood.
>
> A whisp-like and rather appealing young man, who had somehow survived psychologically with the help of his tough/tender elder half-sister, he was a mass of tattoos, at the heart of which was the word MUM.
>
> Like many young people, much of his emotional life revolved around social media, especially his Facebook page through which he appeared to conduct both love affairs and vendettas against his perceived enemies, including, unsurprisingly, the family of the man who had seduced his mother.
>
> Initially the work of therapy consisted mostly of 'being there' at a regular place and time, and providing some flexibility of appointments as his cancellations and rescheduling tested his therapist's commitment and continuity.
>
> Gradually, however, Sean began to face the complexity and fluidity of his feelings about both his parents—fear, rage, love, and confusion. In parallel with this, he began to 'move on' externally. The symbolism and psychological development implied in his changing his job—from chainsaw wielding hedge-trimmer to heavy-goods lorry driver—was evident therapeutically if not to Sean himself. He was no longer, like his father, a 'mad axe man',

but had found an enclosed but private space which could power itself, albeit at the price of dragging behind it some very heavy burdens.

In the virtual setting of therapy, with external reality bracketed off, the interpersonalised inner world comes to the fore as a zone of experimentation and possibility. Lacking such an inner world, the individual is trapped in a thicket of *things*. This 'thing-ness' is highlighted in attachment theory's differentiation between 'teleological thinking' and mentalizing. Teleology—as defined by Fonagy et al. (2002)—describes an 'if this, then that', universe where minds are bypassed, and life amounts to no more than a series of billiard-ball consequential actions and reactions. This teleology is 'pre-mentalizing', prevalent in insecure attachment, while mentalizing, as we shall discuss in more detail later, is a key feature of secure attachment.

> For Sean, the stark and almost unbearable facts of 'my dad killed my mum and now I have got no one', began, as therapy took hold, to be replaced with thoughts like 'my dad didn't know what he was doing, he just went into a blind murderous rage, and now he's crippled with remorse'. 'He and I can at least share our grief.' 'I know what it's like to feel jealousy, because when my girlfriend went off with my best friend I think I could have killed her—or better still him! But thank goodness I didn't.'

Transitional space—which I am here recruiting also as a spiritual zone—the intermediary between external 'teleological' reality and the inner world of fluidity and feelings, is where these thoughts first find their voice. It's here that we feel alive, creative, and satisfyingly related to those around us. Arguably, the technology of social media and the internet compromise this space. Either reality impinges so strongly that selfhood is suppressed as we become data-driven automata, or reality itself is swept away in postmodern anything-goes confusion so that the taste and feel and joke-filled conversation of present-moment breakfast is replaced by envy-provoking Instagram images of smashed avocado. The role of psychotherapy—alongside non-institutional religion and the arts—is as an adult adventure playground, a location where the spirit of existence can flourish, lost worlds be recaptured.

Despite Freud's (1933a) warning that psychoanalysis for the middle aged and beyond was a waste of time, elders increasingly seek help from therapists. But why would mature individuals devote time and money and emotional energy to such a questionable enterprise? Pure self-indulgence? Pandering to middle-class angst? Boredom and frustration? Why not join a political party, environmental group, orchestra, bridge club—or church? Cultivate one's garden and read a novel? So-and-so is 'in' therapy, as one casually says. Yet that little preposition points, at least in part, to the beginnings of an answer. 'Into' implies movement—towards new space, physical and mental. The consulting room, even if virtual, as it is for many in these post-Covid times, is indeed located in actual space-time: a regular fifty minutes of one's life, free from activity other than thoughtful conversation, in a warm room, protected from interruptions and intrusions. Among the mundane hurly-burly of everyday 'living and partly living', a set-aside of one hour or more each week is a haven, not unlike the successions of weekly church attendance or daily monastic prayer.

The location of the self

Prayer-like, therapy opens a door into the mind's inner spaces. But where *is* that inner land, the self's living room? As clients sit at the start of their therapy session, I see their heads angling, turning, eschewing direct gaze, averting or even closing their eyes as they speak while I try to follow their elusive, ever changing trains of thought. Freud used the train metaphor to capture the essence of free association, likening it to looking out of the window in a moving railway carriage (an example of how prevailing technology colours the metaphors scientists draw on).

> An elderly doctor patient was troubled by geological layers of guilt and a sense of failure. 'My mind seems momentarily blank today, although as I look at the Zoom screen I see the word "admit X". In the pre-Covid days it would have been you the therapist who was "admitting" me to your room; am I now to "admit" to my faults, failing, guilt, and misdemeanours? Oh, here comes an association, I'm reminded of a colleague, a friend of a friend, who wrote a best-selling book about his work as a neurosurgeon with its punning title, *Admissions*. That's what doctors do when they

"admit" patients into hospital, but also what one does when one owns up to one's faults and failings. I'm envious of its success—*my* work will never reach the general public in that way.' 'Yes,' responds the therapist, 'I suspect your convention-trammelled mother gave you a sense that you were never quite good enough to help her overcome her own sense of an unfulfilled life.'

These inner non-propositional thoughts fuse words, feelings, and images into an amalgam—a 'sense'—that becomes available for expression and mutual examination with the therapist. In this case, among others, the anxiety of the therapeutic encounter and being 'put on the spot' that blanks out the mind; a well of guilt and self-dislike waiting to be drawn to the surface; feelings of envy and a sense of failure; narcissistic self-preoccupation in which relationships are held at bay. The inner world as seen here is an underworld, a limestone cave beneath the everyday surface of life. The therapist's job is to look at the inaccessible back of their begetter's heads, make patterns out of them, linking them with other seemingly unrelated trains of thought. The aim is to enhance coherence, without sacrificing complexity, to widen the scope of information that informs one's sense of self, one's feelings, and one's actions in the world.

Together, within an overall framework of understanding of human development and its vicissitudes, patient and therapist begin to fashion a story, a meaning, a sense-making narrative about what 'matters', which in turn will stimulate further inner reflections. The process of therapy shines a light into this darkness, illuminates the contours and accretions, unearths the shapes, misshapes, and hieroglyphs that have accumulated in a lifetime of vicissitude, so that, seen from top-down, the subject can say, reality-reinforced, now therapy-triangulated, 'This is, was, and unless I do something about it, will be, my life.'

Psychotherapy in wider cultural space

We come now to psychotherapy's third space—its position in the network of social institutions that make up complex societies. My argument is that psychotherapy plays a crucial but ambiguous role in contemporary culture. In the therapy room the normal social structures of power, authority, hierarchy, information dissemination, patriarchy, moral censure, and manipulation are set aside. Under this moratorium, therapy hovers somewhere between the realms of private and familial relationships, only distantly shaped by laws and contracts, if at all.

Pre-Revolution France designed the 'three estates': the clergy, the nobility, and the common people. In the pre-modern era the tension between temporal and spiritual powers meant that a church, cathedral, or priory was a sacred space where outsiders could take refuge, sequestered from the full strictures of society and the law. The murder of Thomas Becket on Henry II's orders was particularly heinous because it violated the sanctity of Canterbury Cathedral. This sense persists even in the modern era: during the dying days of the Honecker regime in East Germany dissidents met in churches relatively free from the spying and oppression of the Stazi.

Emotional literacy

In Bernard Schlink's novel *The Reader*, Nazi soldiers set fire to a church where French women and children are hiding, based on a true event that epitomised the senseless brutality of war, but with an added sadistic element. The story, starting from Germany in the 1940s, centres on a young Nazi woman, desperate to hide the fact that she is illiterate. She seduces a vulnerable young man, and then by post-coitally asking him to read to her, fills in the gaps in her limited understanding of the world and its words.

For Schlink, the illiteracy of the brutalised Nazi protagonist is a symbol of the emotional wasteland of fascism. 'The reader', the sexually enthralled young man, is a quasi-therapist, but is himself corrupted by the fascist environment which he co-inhabits. He is inevitably affected and marked by his encounter with the woman. After the war, depressed and lonely, observing her post-war Nuremberg-type trial, he takes on the responsibility and guilt which she repudiates. His position is a metaphor for the simultaneous marginalisation and indispensability of psychotherapy, whose project is to promote emotional and social 'literacy'. To do so, it immerses itself in the very confusion and destructiveness which it aims to cure, and by which, like Shakespeare's dyer's hand, it is, to an extent, tainted and contaminated (Shakespeare, sonnet 111).

Struggling with this paradox, the various types of psychotherapy position themselves differently. CBT firmly locates pathology in the client, whose difficulties it aims to redress with straightforward task-setting and suggestion. From that perspective, those who do not seek or need therapy occupy an unquestioned normality—or, possibly, 'normosis' (Bollas, 2019). Classical psychoanalysis, and to an extent its Kleinian progeny, adopt a more tragic worldview in which 'illness' is ubiquitous and inherent in the human condition unless mitigated by psychoanalytic insight. Relational psychoanalysis, and to some extent the Bowlbian attachment-informed therapy espoused here, see emotional illiteracy in the context of a Voltairean trauma-model in which man is born free, but all too often enchained by social forces of abuse and deprivation.

Psychotherapist as fool

Another psychoanalytic precursor is the role reversal implicit in carnivals, festivals, and in satirical figures such as the Shakespearean fool. Established power structures rely on these frolics as a safety valve, but they also call into question the legitimacy of rulers and can be a bridgehead leading to change and democratisation. In the traditional mental hospitals which prevailed when I began my psychiatric life there was an annual Christmas party in which the inmate-patients sat at the 'high table' and were waited upon by the medical director and his (*sic*) staff. Today psychiatric patients live in 'the community' (sadly all too often a euphemism for bleak and lonely social housing) and are championed as 'experts by experience', often by parties anxious to de-marginalise their own political position.

By the very virtue of his social impotence and outsider status, King Lear's fool can mock, reprimand and abrade the King in ways prohibited to his underlings in the power system. Only the Fool can tell Lear what a fool *he* is and 'scape whipping'. Ironically though, the Fool is only able to confront his master with his absurdities and self-delusions because they know each other so well—as the Duke of Wellington said, 'No man is a hero to his valet.' This insider/outsider position enables the Fool to speak truth to power and get away with it. Similarly, the ambiguous role of therapists gives licence to confront clients with their darker, destructive, and self-destructive aspects which in normal life they would rather not think about, let alone discuss. In the world of inner complexity with which therapists deal, delving into this shadow side enables clients to negotiate the pitfalls of living with more nuanced, all-encompassing, and coherent perceptions and assumptions.

During my training, two of my most influential teachers neatly exemplified this outsider/insider role. One came from Mauritius and had lived in the UK since his early twenties but retained a faint French accent. The other's parents were refugees from Nazi Germany, bringing him to the UK aged eight. Educated in England, he too retained a faint accent—in his case German. Both were utterly assimilated and entirely fluent in the English language and mores. However, when these master therapists interviewed clients, their 'foreign' accents and cigar-smoking gestures markedly increased in salience. They became mini-Sigmunds to whom their clients could reveal all because their therapists' demeanour somehow denoted and endorsed an outsider status. This in turn made clients feel that their revelations were in safe keeping, and that, like themselves, the therapist knew what it was to feel an outsider both to themselves and to their prejudicial surroundings.

Insider/outsider ambiguity

But this insider/outsider role is inherently unstable. Therapists crave social acceptance and professionalisation comparable to that afforded to other members of the helping professions: nurses, social workers, doctors, teachers. At the same time, by incorporation into the dominant social discourse they risk losing the *point d'appui* which gives them their unique power.

In our era of disenchantment, religion and psychotherapy have in common this ambiguous social role, with its attendant dangers and opportunities. Archbishops, with their God-given place in the House of Lords, sometimes reprimand political leaders. But without external scrutiny the possibilities for exploitation and malpractice are rife. Priests sexually abuse their parishioners; orphaned children can be preyed on; new age gurus can take advantage of their position and charisma to seduce their followers. Sexual abuse by psychotherapists of patients is likewise a recognised hazard, as is financial exploitation

(Gabbard & Lester, 1996). Fee-insistent analysts can bankrupt their clients, with little discernible mental health benefit, as in the famous Chestnut Lodge Osheroff case (Aviv, 2022). Sadly, even among supposedly self-aware psychotherapists, some of this goes on 'in good faith', with perpetrators genuinely believing that their exploitative actions are beneficial.

These aberrations aside, even mainstream psychotherapy illustrates the tension inherent in living with one foot in the unformulated inner world and the other aiming to impact the secular world of everyday living. Freud claimed he was founding a new science. But, plagued by prevailing anti-Semitism, rather than joining the academic and intellectual mainstream and finding a place in medical or psychology university departments, psychoanalysts became intellectually isolated, founding their own institutes, running their own trainings, and developing notions of psychoanalytic research that diverged from generally accepted standards of evidence and experimentation.

Psychoanalytic psychotherapy continues to veer between cult-like secret societies with a sequestered 'torah' (including detailed study of all twenty-three volumes of the Master's writings and his 'laying-on-of-hands' successors and secret ring-giving), and a yearning for public acceptance. Psychoanalysts are both revered and feared, sought after and marginalised.

In the 1950s and 1960s, especially in the US, psychoanalysis formed the dominant psychiatric and psychological discourse. With the 1970s oil crisis, and the need to cut back on economic profligacy, and the unco-incidental advent of CBT, everything changed. Alongside the 'decade of the brain', the focus of therapy moved from the need to acknowledge and live with subversive dark-side unconsciousness to broad-daylight consciousness. Neurotic suffering was now characterised in terms of errors of logic and inference. In ways that psychoanalysis had failed to address, Beck (1975) and his successors grasped that funding and public recognition depended on the need to conform to conventional research procedures if their therapies were to be validated as effective and efficacious. They made their trainings briefer, their theories less arcane, and focused on alleviating symptoms rather than the whole-person ethical and developmental outcomes which were psychoanalysis's stock in trade.

In this sense therapy has become commodified: a procedure in which patients exchange symptom-reduction for money, either through direct payment or third-party funding from insurance agencies or governments. Comparable degradation of care, kindness, and creativity into utilitarian exchange can be found in contemporary medical and educational systems—CBT contributes to GDP—the gross domestic product which is the apogee of capitalist economic systems (Hickel, 2021). In the eyes of the 'Fourth Estate' (i.e. the media), CBT is now a brand, in which it and the wider world of psychotherapy are conflated, just as sweet fizzy drinks tend to be referred to as Coke, or vacuum cleaners Hoovers.

With this move from the subversive periphery into the mainstream, something vital has been lost. This something—again, let's call it 'spirit'—is what psychoanalytic psychotherapy, for all its convoluted theorising and ancestor worship, manages to capture and embody. This spirit of psychotherapy includes: acknowledgement of and encounter with the sheer irreducibility of complex systems; the inescapability of the negative aspects of human nature—aggression, envy, destructiveness—which need to be identified and confronted before they can be transcended; the role of un-knowing, uncertainty, and surprise; the social-relational as opposed to the individualistic perspective vis-à-vis our own species but also the natural world; a developmental and emergent view of ourselves as opposed to fixed and ahistorical identities; and, last, an implicit or explicit ethic of what it means to flourish and lead a good life.

CHAPTER 5

Spirituality as therapy

Thus far my aim has been to foreground some possible spiritual dimensions of psychotherapy. Contrariwise, this chapter now explores the therapeutic aspects of spirituality. The context of the chapter is a qualitative study carried out by the author consisting of in-depth interviews with people from different faith backgrounds. (For details of the methodology see Appendix). The focus of the interviews was not so much the substance of the subjects' beliefs, especially not their validity or otherwise, but the part that religion and their faith had played and continued to play in their lives. I was especially interested in how their faith had—or had not—helped them deal with the besetting difficulties, setbacks, and traumas of everyday life. My aim was to explore how the 'outcomes' of religious belief and practice overlap with those that derive from the attachment-informed psychoanalytic approaches which comprise my own core beliefs and praxis (cf. Holmes & Slade, 2017).

As with spirituality itself, defining our key word, therapy, is contentious and far from simple. The term derives from Greek/Latin *therapea*, and implies healing of a wound, an illness, a disorder.

Healing comes from old English *haelen*, to make whole, to cure, to *save*. *Salvation* is a key concept in Abrahamic religions. Salvation implies cleansing, making whole, a rescuing from—as my Friston-influenced (Friston, 2010) perspective sees it—the entropic disruptions of what is called 'sin'. God calls the shots, provides an overall narrative of health and moral illness, and points the way to recovery.

Health and healing

No living human has escaped an episode of healed woundedness or recovered ill-health, whether trivial or life-threatening. Try as she might, Sleeping Beauty could not avoid pricking herself on a sewing needle. Cuts, scrapes, infections, fractures, various forms of organ dysfunction or failure are integral to being and staying alive, as, no less, are various degrees of psychological loss, setbacks, fears, phobias, traumas, and psychotic episodes, whether transient or entrenched.

For our discussion two aspects of this are relevant. First, bodies have an array of ways—physical, immunological, behavioural—in which they protect, repair, and heal themselves; these are built in to the evolutionary project of vitality. Second, as a social species, and given the intense vulnerability of its young, human healing is almost always an interpersonal process. Illness generates its arcane sociological rituals: the shaman gyrates, shakes bones, incantates. In the Western world the nursing hand presses the poultice; vaccines jab; wounded surgeons wield the healing knife; tumour- or virus-targeted antibodies are devised by researchers and technicians and delivered by an eager—if exhausted—health workforce. All these speak to the collective commitment of our species to maintaining life in the face of the ever-pressing forces of social and planetary entropy.

Minds, like bodies, veer between integrity and various forms of disintegration. 'Ruptures', major or minor, which threaten the wholeness and happy functioning of our affective mind-world are inevitable. Sadness, misery, anxiety, numbness, delusion—nothing human is alien to our fragile minds. And like its fellow organs, the mind-brain often struggles to balance competing capacities. The immune system needs to respond vigorously to incoming pathogens but not overreact lest allergies and autoimmune illnesses result. The heart ups its output when exercising, but needs must ward off arhythmias or unstoppable tachycardias. Comparably, the mind's job is to balance altruism against self-preservation, exploration against security, risky novelty-seeking against comfort-zone safety, independence against the need to rely on others, creativity against delusional imaginings. We are all, moment to moment, navigating psycho-physiological pathways through the competing demands of wants, needs, and the adjudicating hand of reality (Barrett, 2018).

As with the body, the mind has ways of repairing itself. Sleep, balm of hurt minds, knits up the ravelled sleeve of care. Rest ensures that new days will dawn on diminished or reconsidered troubles. From an evolutionary group selection point of view, when faced with sudden status-loss or bereavement, it can be adaptively advantageous to withdraw and remain *hors de combat* for a while, even at the expense of transient or even more long-lasting depression (Abed & St John-Smith 2022). Anxiety leads to avoidance of perceived danger, albeit if life-expanding experience is thereby jeopardised.

Everyday ruptures are generally quickly repaired. The abandoning parent returns from a seemingly interminable phone call; unpalatable food is replaced with something yummy; the 'grown-ups' can glue together a broken toy; difficult days are transcended with a good night's sleep. Even major trauma can be overcome. Grief runs its course. New beginnings beckon. What's lost is found or replaced. Pastures green succeed bitter winters.

The healing role of religion

The contention of this book is that both religion and psychotherapy form part of the cultural repertoire our species has devised to facilitate and enhance these mind-healing processes. They can be thought of as psychic prostheses, no less potent than the eye- or limb-augmenting technology ranging from spectacles through keyhole surgery to man-made satellites. These prostheses 'bootstrap', in the sense of creating new and expanded niches, extending and transforming the reach of hands, eyes, hearts, and loving attention.

Although the evidence is somewhat mixed, there seems little doubt that religion is good for its adherents' physical and mental health. A Mayo Clinic review showed that:

> Most studies have shown that religious involvement and spirituality are associated with … greater longevity, coping skills, and health-related quality of life (even during terminal illness) and less anxiety, depression, and suicide. (Mueller et al., 2001, p. 16)

However, the study concluded that showing an association between positive health benefits and religion still leaves questions unanswered:

> Although the relationship between religious involvement and spirituality and health outcomes seems valid, it is difficult to establish causality. While religiously involved persons embrace health-promoting behaviors, eschew risky behaviors, and have strong support networks, these factors do not account for all the benefits of religious involvement and spirituality. Rather, these benefits are likely conveyed through complex psychosocial-behavioral and biological processes that are incompletely understood. (Ibid., p. 21)

The focus here are on these 'complex psycho-behavioral processes'. My argument is that although the means differ, the impact of religion and psychotherapy on psychic and mental health are comparable. The aim of this chapter is to describe some of the ways in which religion helps people, and to suggest how, despite very different routes, the desired outcomes of psychotherapy overlap with these.

The search for a secure base

The basic principle of attachment theory is that humans, like our fellow primates, when beset by trauma, illness, exhaustion, and/or threat are psycho-biologically programmed to seek out an 'older, wiser' (Bowlby, 1971) secure-base figure for comfort and protection. 'Secure baseness' implies availability, timely responsiveness, a mentalizing capacity to validate distress, to be consistent and truthful, and to have ways of repairing ruptures (cf. Reibstein, 2023).

Attachment research initially focused on the experiences of infants and small children when separated from their parents, but subsequent studies showed that the attachment dynamic applies across the life cycle, and that adults when threatened are no less drawn to their secure base figure—parent, child, partner, pet, or psychotherapist—than are children. This principle has far-reaching consequences for mental health. To take but one example, Brown and Harris's (1978) pioneering studies of urban working-class mothers showed that frequency of contact with an intimate other was a key feature of relationships that protected subjects from stress-induced depression brought on by poverty and multiple child-rearing.

For children the secure base is normally a parent, but, equally, parents themselves are vulnerable to threat and/or illness, and this may compromise their efforts to provide the comfort which their distressed children need. For adults, their secure base may continue to be a parent, but more commonly is a spouse or partner. Pets, siblings, or close friends may also sometimes fit the bill. In older adults the roles may reverse so that the child becomes the parent's secure base; here too the same restrictions about impediments to security-provision may apply.

God as secure base

Turning now to the results of the research, virtually all religious respondents commented on how helpful it was for them to know that God is 'there' for them, especially in times of trouble. Having access to God fulfils many of the features of a secure base: proximity, responsiveness, acceptance, understanding, comfort, and wisdom.

Granqvist (2020) has developed this idea and differentiates what he calls the *correspondence* from the *compensation* pathways to religious belief. In the former, the believer's God is a continuation and expansion of the parental belief system and the general ambiance of parental attachment with which they have grown up. God here is a meta-attachment figure embodying care in an idealised form, drawing on a bank of positive childhood secure-base and rupture–repair experiences.

The *compensation* pathway is typically found in insecurely attached individuals, who report insensitive developmental experiences with parents. They turn to God at times of extreme distress, and are more likely to have had sudden conversion experiences. In compensation mode, the role of God drastically lessens when stress abates. From a psychoanalytic perspective, God here is a 'last resort' attachment figure evoked to help regulate overwhelming distress in the absence of a good internal object, embodying the 'no atheists in foxholes' rubric.

In the compensation epiphany, an individual—typically during adolescence—'discovers' God and finds in him/her the loving care and attention so egregiously missing during their childhood.

> Andy grew up in conditions of severe emotional and material deprivation. His father drank heavily and, to make ends meet and compensate for her husband's profligacy, his mother took on three cleaning jobs, while Andy and his four siblings were left to fend for themselves. His chaotic adolescence and early adulthood were dominated by school absence, drugs, drink, and minor law transgressions.
>
> Then, in his mid-twenties, at a Druidic ceremony at Stonehenge on Midsummer's Night, he suddenly discovered a spiritual connection with nature and the earth's rhythms. Immediately he could see a path forward, in contrast to his formerly directionless and chaotic existence. Through Druidic observance, buttressed with help from Alcoholics Anonymous, he gradually extricated himself from his previous self-destructive life and began to find a focus, meaning, and purpose.

A paradox here was that Andy's sense of stability and security arose out of his recognition of the transience and mutability of things. By allying himself with the cycle of the seasons, and acknowledging our interdependence with the natural world, he achieved a degree of stability and fixedness of purpose which his chaotic and neglectful upbringing had so signally failed to provide.

The attachment dynamic and the role of the secure base are integral to our psycho-biological heritage. Just as we share seven cervical vertebrae with giraffes, so our primate mind/brain system has a built-in threat/comfort-seeking system, shaped by the hyper-social nature of our species. Ask a group of people to whom what or where they turn for comfort when unwell or traumatised, and virtually none will find the question incomprehensible. Family, friends, and pets are the top triad. Sometimes it is an action, substance, or cultural phenomenon: resorting to alcohol or drugs, listening to favourite music or TV show, having a 'duvet day', going for a walk, going for a run, or digging the garden.

A second aspect is the fact that these secure base strategies are not infallible, and some indeed are self-defeating. Mum doesn't always answer the child's call; the TV may be on the blink; excessive alcohol may exacerbate the very problems it is invoked to alleviate. When attachments are secure however, these temporary setbacks are readily overcome, and the rupture–repair process may serve to strengthen resilience. Where attachment is insecure, especially if disorganised, the sequence is compromised. Here the best hope is the compensation pathway, either towards spiritual awakening, or the long and uncertain process of psychotherapeutic amelioration.

In the 'still face paradigm' (Tronick & Gold, 2020) the caregiver—usually mother—is seated near a four-month-old baby at a 45 degrees angle to a mirror. Preverbal, but highly communicative, such a child is typically supported by intense mother-infant facial and vocal interactions. The mother is then asked to 'freeze' her face for one minute—a long time in the life of a baby. As the seconds pass, the child becomes confused, distressed, and regressed, and 'collapsed', physically and emotionally. But once the minute is up and rupture repaired, children later classified as secure will rapidly re-establish connection with their caregiver, their misery forgiven and forgotten. By contrast, insecure infants when released from maternal face-freeze, will often continue with gaze aversion, and/or resort to self-soothing through scrutinising instead their own images in the mirror.

These differing rupture–repair responses are emblematic of Granqvist's correspondence and compensation pathways to religious succour. We can think of God as the epitome and idealised summation of a secure base, either as actually experienced in the correspondence pathway, or as desired and conjured up in the compensation pathway. But even God, like a real mother, is sometimes 'unavailable'. As in Mark's gospel the supplicant cries to Jesus, 'I believe, Lord, help thou my unbelief' (Mark 9:24); and perhaps echoing this, a contemporary Christian Archbishop of Canterbury, Justin Welby, confessed: 'there are moments when you think "Is there a God. Where is God?"' (*Guardian*, September 18, 2014).

The sociology of medical care

If God is the ultimate secure base, are there comparable processes at work in the sociology of psychotherapy? Granqvist argues that, across countries, there is an inverse relationship between the decline of religion and the rise of welfarism. Over the past half century, religious observance in his native Sweden has been in decline, while the welfare state is ascendent; the converse is true of the US. But this reciprocal relationship is asymmetric: there are aspects of religion which welfarism fails to provide.

US subjects given a subliminal God 'prime' were, despite this operating entirely below consciousness, more likely to undertake exploratory tasks than those exposed to neutral primes and had greater cognitive access to a sense of protection and welfare. Swedish subjects failed to replicate this when exposed to welfare primes, whether supra- or subliminally. The author concludes that 'the welfare system does not fit the mental model of interpersonal others, such as that of an attachment figure, for which the mind has been designed' (Granqvist, 2020, p. 330).

The implications of this study have a bearing on the design not just of psychotherapy services but of social and medical services in general. In the UK, patients no longer have a personal relationship with their primary care physician (GP). When symptoms arise, it is assumed that any suitably qualified doctor will do, despite evidence that continuity of care with a known physician (i.e. a secure base figure) reduces hospital referrals, diminishes healthcare costs, and improves medical outcomes (Whitaker, 2021).

In a similar vein, current mental health and social services typically operate on a 'hot desk' system, so the benefits of clients from week to week being seen in the same room and at the same time by the same person are often ignored. Again, it is wrongly assumed that what matters is an impersonal form of 'welfare', not the person or the physical context in which it is provided. Indeed, post-Covid, the patient–GP relationship has changed from one that generally had the features of secure attachment— timely responsiveness to distress, intimate knowledge over time leading to epistemic trust—to an avoidant pattern in which both care seeker and care provider are guarded and self-protective (Elder, 2023).

Specificity

All this speaks to the specificity of the attachment relationship. For a distressed child 'only Mum' or 'Dad'—however compromised their caregiving capacities—will do. As Bowlby (1971) pointed out, for adults who have lost a lover, the consoling cliche that 'there are plenty more fish in the sea' is of scant comfort. A bureaucratic 'service provider' is not relationally oriented to address distress. In these circumstances, attachment theory posits that part of the reason health and social services are so overwhelmed with need is that the very attempt to 'manage' demand increases it. If attachment needs are not assuaged, the search for security remains supercharged and feeds into medical recidivism.

God by contrast works because he/she is always '*my* God', an all-powerful symbol of one who knows the believer from the inside out, back to front, and from start to finish. Likewise, a therapist can and will over time begin to take on the features of a secure base. Initially there is a concrete aspect to this—the physical personhood of the therapist, her tone of voice, specific room, time, and day all assume secure base ambiance. Where this is problematic, as it will be for disorganised 'borderline' clients, the lack of secure base-ness experience and therefore expectation—rigid sticking to session times, absence of responsiveness in between—reinforce a sense that 'nobody really cares' but can, given sufficient flexibility, over time be addressed and redressed (Bateman, 2022; Holmes & Slade, 2017).

> Gradually the 'therapeutic' aspects of the therapist become abstracted and internalised, an inner presence which the patient can call upon when needed. When things are going well, the need for intermediary help can also be invoked. An inner voice—God's or that of a therapist—might insist that: '... this is more than I/we can manage on my/our own—you need some additional help—a trip to hospital, a discussion with your partner, the housing department, careers advisor, etc.' This truth is encapsulated in the joke about the supplicant who repeatedly prays to God, 'Please please oh Lord, let me win the lottery,' to be met with silence, until God exasperatedly expostulates, 'OK, I'll try to help, but meet me halfway—at least buy yourself a ticket!'

The therapist/God parallel may at first sight appear tendentious. After all, a therapist is no more than a run of the mill professional hired to help with circumscribed psychological or emotional difficulties—ranging from 'anger management' to trying to decide if one's partner really is 'the one'. But as Garland (2018) so beautifully put it, therapy entails 'taking the non-problem seriously'. A psychological symptom is where therapy starts. But as therapy progresses the 'presenting problem' may appear as no more than an extraneous thread, a jumping off point in a tangled skein which, when unravelled, encompasses a person's whole life story, personality structure, and psychosocial ecology. At the core of this, for the religious, dwells one's relationship to a deity, an entity who comprehends one's strengths, faults, and failings far better than one can oneself. Likewise, a crucial aim of the therapeutic relationship is to reveal the client's self to their self.

Beyond narcissism

This begs the question—who *is* this self to whom the self is revealed? Here the concept of a prime mover God puts a stop to the infinite regress, sidestepping psychotherapy's besetting hazard, the potential for never-ending narcissistic self-preoccupation. According to Neville Symington (1998), a psychoanalyst whose initial career choice was the priesthood, consilience between religion and psychoanalysis lies in their shared focus on the distinction between narcissistic self-preoccupation and 'life-giver' concern for others. In Symington's model, psychoanalysis is an ethical project, helping people to live good lives. For him the essence of this is the Kleinian 'depressive position' in which envy and destructiveness are owned and tempered, in contrast to a life of splitting and projection in which 'badness' is located externally in the let-downers, the enemy, the scapegoat, the disowned, repudiated, and often dehumanised 'other'.

The maturational process

From a free energy perspective, to this ethical take on the narcissism of splitting and self-aggrandisement, we can add an *existential narcissism* in which the world as seen through the eyes of the subject falsely equates one's top-down perceptions with reality. Moving beyond this to an understanding that everything that is external to the self, including the natural world, animate and inanimate, has an existence indepen-dent of oneself is built in to both psychotherapy and many religions.

In the universe of primary narcissism, psychoanalysis hypothesises that infants assume that their mother and her breast exist purely for their own benefit. Moving to a perspective in which people are seen to have their own independent lives and projects is part of healthy maturation. Research suggests that children who have been 'mental-ized' by their caregivers—seen as having desires, beliefs, and projects of their own—rather than as genetic extensions of their parents or even behavioural chess pieces lacking an inner life—find it easier similarly to mentalize others, at school entry and beyond (Allen & Fonagy, 2006). Thinking about this philosophically, Neiman (2016) expounds Kant's maturity triad: having a mind of one's own; being able to put oneself in the other's place and so to see the world—including oneself—from their own point of view; and consistency of judgement.

The psychological space of therapy is conceptualised by Ogden (2016) and others (e.g. Benjamin, 2017) as a 'third'—an innovative, transitional niche which therapist and patient fashion together as a co-created duet for one. As therapy progresses, the patient gets a growing sense of this dyadic triangle—self, therapist, and third. She begins to grasp that the therapist is both 'there' for her benefit and has an inde-pendent existence. For Britton (2015) this developmental model is the contemporary version of the oedipal situation where a child, excluded from her parents' sexual love, begins, in compensation, to develop a mind and life of her own. Beyond the constricted Western nuclear fam-ily, an anthropological take on this (Hrdy, 1999) suggests that it is the role of 'alloparents'—grandparents, aunts, older siblings, cousins—that help children to grasp the multiplicity of points of view, and so take the first steps on the long path to mature mentalizing.

Thirdness

Stepping beyond the limitations of narcissism can also be integral to a religious viewpoint.

> As the proverb tells us, 'The children of lovers are orphans'. Naomi was a shy, overlooked child whose mother and stepfather seemed so wrapped up in each other that they had little time for

her and her half-siblings. One day while walking to school she suddenly noticed a perfectly formed dandelion head, poised to spread its seed. She was struck by what she described, in retrospect, as *a wordless sense of the "whatness" of the flower'*. Here in the natural world was a realm outside herself, indifferent, yet with its own patterns, rules, and beauty. When later in life she trained as a Druidic bard she felt that she drew on this experience and felt that she was finally 'coming home' to nature.

As a child in the presence of natural beauty, with its independent existence, Naomi's misery and feelings of unbelonging evaporated. Unconsciously perhaps, the sexuality of the flower was to be celebrated rather than uncomfortably thrust in her face by her parents' all too evident mutual sexual preoccupation. Momentarily she felt part of something greater than herself, and this paradoxically, led to self-strengthening and individuation.

But although Naomi was dyadically alone with her dandelion in this initial epiphany, a third element was needed to complete the positive triangle: in her case the paganistic rituals of Druidic practice and philosophy. This could be seen as exemplifying the 'compensatory' pathway to spirituality. Naomi's bleak feeling of disconnection in her family was transcended by her discovery of an intellectual and practical framework of reciprocity with her fellow Druids and with planetary rhythms. Sex now was no longer an excluding envy-provoking intrusion, but integral to nature's cycle of fertility, death, and rebirth.

Psychoanalytic therapy is sometimes accused of fostering rather than counteracting narcissism and self-preoccupation, of being the disease of which it purports to be the cure. Although there may be some validity to this charge, it is counterbalanced in two key ways. First, in psychoanalytic work, although the focus is on the individual patient, this is always in the context of relationality. Therapist and patient together 'triangulate'—in the cartographic sense—the patient, her feelings, her life story, and their mutual relationship. Two people are looking at a 'third', even if one of the seekers is part of what is being sought—the patient herself.

Second, brains don't exist in isolation. Attuned caregivers are linked with their offspring, right brain-to-right brain (Schore, 2001), enabling them intuitively to 'know' and respond to their baby's needs. A comparable process applies to adult romantic couples. In a now classic study (Coan et al., 2006), happily married couples were asked to participate in an experiment in which one member was placed in an fMRI scanner and warned that she would receive a mild electric shock to her leg in the subsequent twenty seconds. The study examined three conditions: subject on their own; holding a stranger's hand; and holding their spouse's hand. In each scenario, activation of the stress-responsive hypothalamic–pituitary–adrenal (HPA) network was followed on the scan. Unsurprisingly, the results showed that blood flow to the HPA axis was greatest when the subjects were alone, and least when holding their partner's hand.

From a neuroscience perspective, the partners' brains can be thought of as acting in concert. The scanned subject experiences bottom-up anxiety at the incoming mild trauma. By contrast, with no direct personal threat, the hand-holder is able to process the impending shock in a top-down way by unbound-energy-reducing thoughts, conscious or otherwise: 'I'm here', 'everything will be OK', 'together we'll cope with this' (Coan, 2016; Coan et al., 2006). Two brains spell two-part harmony, like singers in a choir. This division of labour maintains psychic integrity and generates cognitive-affective models enabling smooth adaptation to the environmental conditions subjects find themselves in.

Comparably, one can visualise psychotherapy as a process in which client and therapist gradually and increasingly come to form a 'duet for one' (Friston & Frith, 2015). The client begins to allow formerly repressed or split-off anxiety-laden sensations to surface. This is the essence of Freud's famous free association injunction to his clients to say anything that comes into their mind, however irrelevant-seeming or embarrassing. Free associations generate surprisal in both therapist (via countertransference) and patient. But because the therapist is not directly experiencing the mental pain (like the hand-holding spouse above) she can develop more complex and adaptive models with which to match the incoming sensations.

A therapist will often, via countertransference, vicariously feel a patient's anxiety and lack of trust. Rather than acting on these feelings either with reassurance or rejection, she might translate them into an overall formulation: 'As I see it, your current fears link back to that crucial moment when your mother was admitted to hospital with post-natal depression when you were a baby. Your caregiving aunt struggled to "know" you and so provide the accurate mirroring and containment you needed. The result is that you are constantly on the alert, expecting those close to you suddenly to disappear—or misread you.' (Reasonable enough comment, although perhaps too much of a one-who-knows 'lecture' to be a really creative intervention.)

As this dissolution of narcissistic process progresses the therapist also emerges as a distinct being with her own perspectives and agendas—often painfully evident when therapists make mistakes (as in the lecture/interpretation above), take holiday breaks, become pregnant, suffer illness, or move away. True, the therapist is exclusively 'there' for the patient for the duration of the session, but once the hour is over, the patient is left to deal with separation, loss, and a reminder that she is far from the only pebble on her therapist's beach.

> Eric, a hard-working father of three, sought therapy after the breakdown of his marriage. He had heard on the grapevine that his therapist, like himself, was a divorcee. Although superficially coping with work and his role as a separated father, and temporarily buoyed up by short-term love affairs, he felt alone in the world. His envy of what he saw as successful and happy couples was unbounded. Gradually he came to trust his therapist with his feelings of misery, inadequacy, and rejection. One day he suddenly noticed that his therapist was wearing a wedding ring, and blurted out, 'You've gone and got married without telling me. How dare you!' The therapist pointed out that the ring had been there all along, suggesting that it was only now that Eric was beginning to break out from his envy-averse defensiveness, that he could begin to face such a fact.

A modicum of dyadic trust was needed before Eric could contemplate his therapist's separate existence, and indeed that 'marriage'—with its multiple and complex significance—also had an independent meaning and pattern which was there for him to explore. Eric felt both diminished and strengthened by this. He was diminished in the sense that he saw more clearly that the world—including his former wife—was not there for his benefit. But his perspectives were also expanded because he could see the thread of meaning which ran through his life, and that he had married in an attempt to quell his envy of couples he perceived as happy, rather than out of genuine disinterested love for his wife, and that this in part was what lay at the root of their difficulties.

I'm suggesting here that both in spiritual epiphany and in mutative psychoanalytic work there are overlapping elements which counteract narcissism. First, there is a here-and-now *experiential event* in which the self is confronted with something or someone external to itself—the impress of the dandelion, the wedding ring as Erik suddenly 'saw' it. Second, there is a *self–other context*—Naomi and the natural world, the married therapist and patient—in which the 'otherness' of the other with its independent existence cannot be avoided. Third, there is a *relationship* between these two components, with elements both of relatedness/attachment and separateness/loss. Finally, a binding structure of *independent meaning* is co-created, able to encompass all three elements.

For Naomi this was the sense of her interconnectedness of nature, the understanding that she and her fellow humans are part of and partake in the natural processes of birth, maturation, death, and rebirth. For Eric it was the realisation that the specifics of his misery were no more than particular instances of universal themes—relatedness, separation, love, hate, envy, and gratitude.

The meaning of meaning

Eric's epiphany entailed the conception that 'events'—in his case divorce—have causes and explanations. Psychoanalytic soul-maps, including as in his case oedipal envy, suppressed or acknowledged, can bring objectivity and relief to mental suffering.

> Another interviewee, Pierre, was a bipolar sufferer. His late-adolescent spiritual journey illustrates the ways in which 'finding' God-given meanings can help transcend the fragile omnipotence of narcissism. Pierre's self was built on a sense of his own superiority. His parents were successful artists and musicians. But as an adolescent he became painfully aware that his

talents, non-negligible though they might appear, were meagre in comparison with theirs. As a student, the competitive culture of university reinforced his inner tension between his family sense of specialness and feelings of personal failure.

During an art history exam he found himself distracted and preoccupied with the question 'who made you?' *He* was an artist, his parents were artists, where did *their* art 'come from'?

By the end of the exam he had decided that *there must be a God*. Only this logical formulation—as he experienced it—could answer the question 'who made his makers?', those revered and envied parents. He now saw that beyond his own talents and theirs—musical and artistic—was an all-powerful deity whose powers were unlimited.

His narcissism came up short, but with it there was a huge feeling of peace and relief. Omnipotence was transferred from himself to the deity, and so could remain intact. Instantly relieved of his self-preoccupied depressive misery, Pierre saw himself as a baby, cradled in the arms of a God, rather than struggling with his own flawed sense of supreme worth.

His devotion to the Church for the rest of his life maintained this bulwark against the twin dangers of depression and narcissistic omnipotence.

From a free energy perspective, there's no mystery about meaning. In order to survive and thrive, organisms need to make and continuously remake models of their environment. These models equate to 'meaning' in the sense that they map the organism's surroundings—the creature's *Umwelt*—into patterns and tracks that meet its immediate and projected future needs. 'Meaning' is built into the nerve centres of successful, that is, 'well-adapted' species. Nervous systems, and especially brains, are structured around meanings.

Managing uncertainty

But both organisms themselves and the environments they find themselves in are inherently unstable. Uncertainty constantly challenges pre-existing meanings. The environment is ever-changing, while 'meaning' is essentially a prediction about the persistence and reproducibility of environmental conditions that prevail when the model is devised.

In our species meaning and purpose arise out of connectedness. This applies 'horizontally' to one's surrounding secure base—family group, 'tribe', and natural environment—and 'vertically' across time past and time to come. The latter operates via one's heritage, children and grandchildren, or projects large and small—horticultural, artistic, or musical, grandiose or humble—from repairing a broken plate or assembling an IKEA flatpack, composing a symphony, to going to a prayer meeting or a psychotherapy session.

A food source today is likely to be one tomorrow—but may not! Meanings must encompass the known *and* the unknown—in the famous Rumsfeld formula, the known unknown and unknown unknown. To which, from a psychoanalytic perspective one adds the 'unknown known'—that which one knows bottom-up in one's bones but chooses top-down to ignore.

This dialectic between belief and unbelief, certainty and doubt is, in our age of anxiety and disenchantment, a *fort/da* with which believers struggle with daily. It is built into Christ's Gethsemane doubts when subjected to extreme agony. In fundamentalist Islam no such doubts exist, given that the Koran is held to be the direct dictation of the deity. However, more mystical versions of Islam such as Sufism, and in Judaism the Kabbalah, hold knowing and mystery together so that openness to the unexpected is actively invoked by esoteric ritual. This parallels the psychoanalytic espousal of 'negative capability'—the capacity to tolerate not-knowing within the structure of the psychoanalytic frame. The idea of the mystery and of a power that cannot be named—whether the name of the Almighty, aka J*w*h, or 'the' (i.e. reified) unconscious—apply to both.

Awe and the ineffable

Psychotherapy and spirituality both provide meaning-maps from which much of their power flows, but both at the same time acknowledge the partiality and inadequacy of earth-bound attempts to understand the mysteries of ourselves and the world which contains us. Ineffable experience, whether in a general philosophy of 'more things in heaven and earth …', or in the light of specific spiritual events, plays an important part in many people's advent to religion.

> Paul was a seventy-year-old man for whom 'spirituality' had been a continuing source of comfort through the many vicissitudes of his life. He described how, aged fourteen, as a lonely, emotion-suppressed American adolescent on holiday in Europe, he was left to fend for himself while his 'Great Gatsby' parents caroused with their friends. He tentatively entered Chartres Cathedral and found himself tearfully sensing something 'other, awesome, a direct feeling of the presence of God' which persisted ever since.

The 'found himself' passive voice here is important. Transcendental experiences 'happen to', 'come upon' the subject, rather than being experienced as self-generated, as the poet Stallings (2023) puts it, more like a bat dropping from a tree or rock face into the unknown than a bird pushing off from its perch with a direction already in mind. In attachment terms this epiphany could be seen as a response of a habitually avoidant child, a product of Pilgrim Puritanism, to the subliminal (cf. 'sublime') cues of eternity, grace, and ordered complexity implicit in Gothic architecture. The cathedral evoked the presence of a safe, containing, caring other—the secure base so lacking in Paul's upbringing. This in turn facilitated the emergence of hitherto inaccessible affect, a novel and enduring sense of hope and aspiration.

This formulation is close to the attachment model of spirituality—a subliminal message that instigates 'broaden and build' states of mind (Granqvist, 2006; Mikulincer & Shaver, 2007). By contrast, Freud's (1919h) famous discussion of the 'Uncanny' emphasises the infantile and regressive aspects of non-material, 'oceanic' experience. His paper starts from the German word for uncanny: '*Unheimlich*', that is, un-homely, unfamiliar, uncomfortable, uneasy. With characteristic brio, Freud suggests it is in fact the very 'heimlich'-ness of things, their *familiarity*, the 'I've been through this movie before' feeling, that in such transcendental moments reawakens hitherto repressed affects, especially anxieties. Omens and portents represent repressed wishes, untempered by reality, illustrating for Freud (p. 243) 'the omnipotence of thoughts', 'instantaneous wish-fulfilments', and 'narcissistic overestimation of subjective mental processes'. Freud's psyche here is essentially on its own—the tripartite self wrestling with itself. The spiritually informed perspective advocated here sees 'primitive' perceptions mediated and mitigated interpersonally in the transitional, we-mode zone. Here the uncanniness of the unconscious and the realities of causality negotiate until a consensus, religious, sceptical, or open-minded is reached.

For Freud, from his patriarchal perspective, uncanny experiences were no more than vestiges of infantile thought processes, phylogenetically linked to the 'primitive animism' of pre-modern man. We now know that mystical, paranormal, premonitory, and hallucinatory experiences, of the sort undergone by adolescent Paul above, are widespread, and certainly not confined to the mentally ill or 'primitives', as was formerly thought (Johns & van Os, 2001). Similarly, meaningful coincidences, theorised by Jung (1969) as 'synchronicities', are not uncommonly described or occur in psychotherapy.

As William James (1902) made clear more than a century ago, a distinction needs to be made between the experiential legitimacy of these phenomena, and the explanatory framework that might account for them. A psychotherapeutic fundamental is both the validation of experience, and a concomitant tentativeness in probing its meaning and context.

Psychoanalytic 'interpretations' are by nature hypothetical, tinged with uncertainty—or should be. In the conceptualisation I am advocating, the essence of 'the unconscious' is not a fund of unmetabolised sexuality and aggression as seen in classical psychoanalysis, but its free-energy derived mystery and unknowability. De-pathologising the psychoanalytic project in this way aligns it with the idea of a spiritual realm, in contrast both to pseudo-scientific psychoanalytic certainties, and the simplistic materialism and instrumentalism of neo-liberal culture.

Egoless states

This returns us to Bion's (1967) much invoked injunction to therapists to approach their work 'beyond memory and desire'. The rhetoric of his call is defiantly paradoxical—and dangerously encouraging for would-be 'wild' analysts. After all, remembering and piecing together into a pattern what the patient has said in the service of helping them to create a meaningful narrative of their distress and thus to get 'better', is central to the psychoanalytic project. But, as Ogden (2016) argues, what Bion is really calling for here is a temporary *psychic merging* of patient and therapist, not unlike the 'duet for one' and we-mode already discussed. This requires a temporary suspension of the ego boundaries of both parties, and the cognitive structures which shape them.

From a spiritual perspective, Bion's paradox is that an 'empty mind' is far from empty—merely cleared of preconceptive cant, and therefore open, if only partially and transiently, to a deeper reality. Transcendentalism brings 'news from nowhere': an ego-free region, the 'beyond', a realm inaccessible to the conscious, willing, choosing self. Mysticism implies direct contact with, or access to, the divinity/infinity, an (or the) 'ultimate reality' beyond everyday experience. The Buddhist notion of emptiness exemplifies this attempt to find words to describe the ineffable. Psychoanalysis has its own version of mystical spirituality. Eigen (1998) traces a 'mystical' current in psychoanalytic thinking, drawing particularly on Milner (1987), Winnicott (1992), and again, Bion (1970), each of whom, in different ways, sees the psychotherapeutic encounter and the crucible of the consulting room as sacred places, providing access to authentic and 'ultimate' psychological reality.

For Bion, the apotheosis of the psychoanalytic mysticism we are hinting at is 'O', the impenetrable ground of being from which all knowledge (K), desire, and memory emanate. Ultimate reality is unspeakable, and so can only be designated by symbols, not words: the Talmudic proscription on uttering God's name, and Bion's (1967) 'grid' with its 'alpha function', 'beta elements', etc. Bion links 'O' with 'F', the psychoanalyst's faith in the psychoanalytic process, in life itself, and in the capacity to survive destructiveness and attacks on linking. Bion, a tank commander in the First World War, saw the ability to 'think under fire' as a prerequisite of analytic capability.

While the further reaches of psychoanalytic mysticism may seem remote from everyday psychotherapy practice, two mundane aspects bring home the importance of non-ego states in therapy. The first is the quotidian mystery of dreaming. As dreamers, we cannot fail to be surprised by the complexity, fecundity, and strangeness of dream-life. 'How on earth did I think all that up?' we ask ourselves. 'Who is the dreamer that dreams?' 'From where do dream thoughts come?' The narrative virtuosity of dream-life remains mysterious, despite all the advances in the neuroscience of sleep (Hobson, 2007).

If night dreams are 'spiritual' in the sense that they come from an unpredicted part of the self not encompassed by the conscious ego, so too do the waking dreams or 'reverie' that are integral to psychoanalytic work. Like a writer, the imaginative clinician has to practise the art of being simultaneously awake *and* 'asleep'. She must be alert and alive to the reality of the patient and his story, to the boundaries and parameters of the clinical situation, and the inevitable ending and loss that follows intense connectedness. At the same time she must be able to 'dream' lucidly, in the sense of letting her own thoughts and feelings flow impersonally through her, observing them, holding them in readiness for consideration, first with herself and then with the patient. There is a kind of secular 'reverence' in this 'reverie'. The patient is the focal point around which the therapist's waking-dream thoughts revolve. However ill, destructive, rageful, or even obnoxious the patient may appear, his or her inner world remains the one and only object of focus and interest, and this is an ethical as well as a technical requirement for successful therapy.

Guidance on the spiritual journey

To return to our mantra: two heads are generally better than one. Together, the free energy zone can be faced, rather than fought, fled, or render one frozen. This necessary companion for the religious is a deity, together with the priest, guru, or wise person able to mediate between the sublime and the mundane. Likewise, in psychotherapy the therapist is the needed free energy minimising companion, able and willing to throw a 'beam of intense darkness' (Grotstein, 2007) into the psychic unknown. Therapists have—or should have—two sets of specialist knowledge and skills to carry them through this process. First, they have 'been there before', in their own training therapy, and in the countless journeys with patients that they have undertaken and learned from. They know the territory and have a set of meta-narratives that can encompass at least some of the unminimised energy which threatens their patients' psychic integrity. They also will be aware of the limitations of their knowledge, be able to grant that every individual has their unique untouchable moiety of free energy, or as Freud puts it:

> There is often a passage in even the most thoroughly interpreted dream which has to be left obscure; this is because ... during the work of interpretation ... there is a tangle of dream-thoughts which cannot be unravelled ... *this is the dream's navel, the point in which it reaches down into the unknown.* (1900a, p. 525, italics added)

Or in Winnicott's (1992) version, the therapeutic work of stripping away the false self still leaves an 'inviolable core self' that mother and analyst needs must respect. The good enough parent accepts their child's monosyllabic grunt when asked 'How was your day at school?', knowing that the truth will emerge given time. Similarly, the therapist will not press for the details of her patient's trauma until the moment comes for speaking the unspeakable.

This brings us to the second aspect of psychotherapy practice that further approximates spiritual and psychoanalytic perspectives. Winnicott's transitional space is a vital no man's land between the inner world of phantasy and external reality, the play area between the 'facts' of our existence and the inner world of phantasmagorical experience. Free energy both threatens and liberates our psychic life. It is dangerous because it can overwhelm and disrupt psychic equilibrium. It is liberating because, if quelled, tamed—*bound*—it leads to better understanding and a more adaptive relationship to the prevailing environment—which in our species' case consists mainly of our fellow humans.

In transitional space ideas can be tried out, alternative scenarios enacted, possibilities considered, top-down models via embodied cognition (Seth, 2022) refined, so that they more nearly approximate to the truths of our being-in-the world. Is that a sick bird or flapping black plastic? Let's get nearer, look more closely, find out the true state of affairs (Holmes, 2020). Does this feeling in my chest mean that I really love him? But are these feelings to be trusted? Are my top-down models, forged in infancy, pushing me down familiar pathways of oedipal infatuation, rejection, and despair?

However, this theorising remains firmly within a transcendentalist Cartesian dualistic world in which body and soul are seen as separate.

Today, combining the idea of embodied cognition (we think with our bodies, our gestures, with our 'gut feelings' as well as our minds) with a revival of a more immanent world-as-sacred approach to spirituality, psychotherapy can provide a different perspective on such mystical moments. In his penultimate work, Freud (1939a) seems to have moved beyond his former vision of religion as mere illusion, and begin to acknowledge its valid healing properties. Black (2006) and Wright (2006) trace the 'maternalistic' movement in psychoanalysis from Freud's rejection of submission to the punitive oedipal *'nom-du-pere'* father, to a celebration of playful preverbal love between mother and child, extending outwards to a reverence for the natural world and beyond.

Winnicott saw religion, art, and psychoanalysis as occupying a cultural transitional play-space, located in the intermediate zone between creative wishfulness and the strictures of reality. Blass (2023) too suggests that Freud (1939a) himself was already reaching towards this idea in *Moses and Monotheism*. In this end-of-career work Freud suggests that his Moses-was-an-Egyptian theory could be wrong in historical fact and yet somehow right at an emotional level. From the neuroscience perspective adopted here, transitional space is free-energy space—where top-down preconceptions meet bottom-up immediate sensory experience and grapple with their discrepancies. The evolutionary role of transitional space is to draw on dream-like creativity to find better models to accommodate resultant free energy. The challenge for religion, art, and psychotherapy is to steer a course between dogmatism and rigidity on the one hand and chaos, incomprehensibility, or psychosis on the other—and to know the difference.

In the consulting room, holding onto hope, and communicating, despite despair, that 'this too will pass' combine as essential psychotherapeutic qualities. The therapist must deploy her capacity for secure attachment, with its in-built flexibility and responsiveness in the face of the rigidity and black-and-whiteness of play-deprived insecure patterns of attachment.

Developmental narratives

We live in a world of labels. Like designer clothing, we wear our identities on our sleeves. We are 'addictive', 'on the spectrum', neuro-atypical, PTSD or ADHD sufferers, 'challenged', LGBT, in search of 'people who look like me', 'lower/upper middle class'. Much of this is good and necessary. Our brains have evolved to classify and differentiate. We need to pick out foe from friend; what's good to eat and what to avoid; to whom we can bestow epistemic trust and whose advice it's best to question or out-of-hand reject. And such identities reveal the power structures which underlie their former invisibility—discrimination, colonialisation, marginalisation, exploitation, and prejudice.

But there is a down side. Militant identity labelling can distract from the developmental processes which have led to it. Who we are is a moving target as we progress along life's journey (Parfit, 1984). Ironically, the complex historical social processes that underpin, say, racism or homophobia, can be obscured by the potencies of specific labels. Similarly, a 'mental health' label, 'neurodiverse' say, can obfuscate the complex interactions of genetics, environmental influence, agency, and cruel or benign chance that go to make up an individual life. In addition, the new science of epigenetics suggests that social forces impact even at a cellular level on the individual life story.

These difficulties increasingly affect and afflict the world of mental health. Notoriously, each succeeding edition of the US *Diagnostic and Statistical Manual* (DSM) adds to the burgeoning list of psychiatric illnesses or 'conditions'. Fine tuning does bring benefits—it is worth knowing that Bipolar 1 is more severe and life-threatening than is Bipolar 2. However, in the US there is a significant commercial aspect to such labelling: health insurance companies, who have a vested interest in DSM, adjust their premiums accordingly. More importantly, there is a danger that overemphasis diagnosis or pseudo-diagnosis inhibits the developmental perspectives inherent in a psychoanalytic approach to mental health.

For psychotherapists the developmental history of the traumatised person is as important as the trauma itself in determining the outcome of the PTSD. The idiographic meaning of the trauma and how it fits into a person's subsequent life story will play a big part in recovery or otherwise. Quoting Nietzsche, Winnicott asserts that all trauma is secondary: 'the dreadful has already happened'.

Sheila developed PTSD following a car accident. Her physical injuries were minor, but thereafter she felt extremely anxious and unsafe in cars, cripplingly worried whenever her children were travelling, and mistrustful of all drivers. Given her peripatetic work, and 'soccer mum' role, this had a major negative impact on her life. But the consequences of this random accident did not, from a developmental perspective, come out of the blue. Psycho-analytically, the trauma was traumatic because it reignited stored but unprocessed memories of previous blows.

A turning point had come in Sheila's childhood when, aged eleven, without preparation, her mother picked her up from school and announced that they were moving to a new house—her mother's lover's—and Sheila was from that moment on to have a new father and a new school. No explanation or discussion was offered. Her trust in teachers and parents never fully survived this episode. She became a school refuser as she embarked on teenage rebellion encompassing extreme left-wing politics and a powerful identification with victims of powerlessness and oppression. Her hitherto unprocessed anxiety about sudden adverse change—for which she had no top-down model or borrowed brain with whom to co-process it—erupted in response to the car crash, and, despite a course of trauma-focused CBT, never fully subsided.

The developmental-contextual approach is in danger of being lost, not just in psychiatry but in medicine more widely. The secure base figure is the guardian of a child's developmental history. Mum above all others will remember what sort of baby her child was—fussy, placid, ravenous, giggly, etc. Football-mad dad will recall when his teenage son first kicked a ball aged three. Cherished family photographs are a store of cradle-to-grave memories. There are echoes here of pre-problematic primary care medicine. The 'family doctor', as a surrogate secure base, would 'know' her patients, their families, and their illnesses over long periods, often extending to three generations. She would have visited the family home, seen its constraints and social milieu, and so be alert to the contextual meaning of her patients' symptoms. In our increasingly bureaucratised world all this is in danger of being lost. A family doctor's implicit knowledge was an invaluable temporal map of a patient's life trajectory against which specific illness episodes could be evaluated. The GP's internal monologue might run something like:

> This chap *never* comes to the surgery; we must take his abdominal pain seriously. Mmm, I remember now, his mother died of stomach cancer when she was not much older than him, so his symptoms *could* be something minor but calling up unresolved grief about her. Nevertheless we must make sure he has a proper gastroscopy and MRI scan before going down the reassurance/counselling route.

If psychoanalytic psychotherapy is the last bastion of developmentalism as opposed to identity medicine, where does spirituality, which might seem to imply an inner kernel of self unaffected by the externals of aging and social change, fit in? For Abrahamists, God transcends space and time and so can see into the past as well as the future and so monitor our life track. Buddhism and paganism are in touch with the cycles of nature—birth, growth, flowering, maturation, decay, death, and Persephonic renewal. For several of the interviewees in the study of religion's role in everyday life, a narrative of spiritual development—the story of the subjects' religious journey—formed an important part of their identity. This typically entailed reconsidering the 'correspondence' religion with which they grew up, and moving in a 'compensation' direction in a form of spiritual reorganisation. There was a clear therapeutic aspect to these stories, comparable to those which psychotherapy aims to achieve.

> Roger had grown up in a conventional 'C of E' environment, in which, on pain of physical punishment from his rigid and rejecting father, he dutifully went to church on Sundays and made the expected obeisance. Following in his father's footsteps, he trained as a surgeon. Then, aged twenty-nine, he became embroiled in a crisis, when he noticed and made public his conviction that the consultant under whom he was training was neglecting his NHS duties in favour of his private practice. However, this 'whistle-blowing' led not to a cleansing of the situation and investigation of the senior, but 'gaslighting', in which Roger himself was

accused of making unsupported accusations and suffering from mental illness. He was suspended from his job and sought help from his local priest. This kind man validated Roger's qualms, comparing his accusations about his boss to Christ overturning the tables in the temple. This led to a surge of self-confidence in which Roger decided on a different, albeit less well remunerated career as a priest himself (a more benign version of his father-figure transference), and switched Churches to a more funda-mentalist, actively celebratory form of Christianity.

As with Sheila's dreadful-has-already-happened trauma, for Roger, encountering the corrupt 'senior' summoned up largely unconscious procedural memories of his unloving father. The helpful priest point-ing to a more loving God seemed to have a healing effect which, had it occurred in the context of psychotherapy, would have been deemed a positive outcome.

A similar experience of disillusionment and psychic reorganisation within the framework of religion is illustrated by Esther:

> Esther, a successful solicitor, who grew up in an orthodox Jewish family. With two high-flying older brothers she felt that she had slipped unnoticed under the parental radar. She was very devout and followed religiously her prescribed roles. When the time came for an arranged marriage she had some doubts. She asked God to guide her. When she dreamed of a beautiful flower-bedecked marriage bed she took this as divine endorsement of the match. However, the marriage proved to be a disaster. Her ultra-orthodox husband was abusive of her and controlling of their children and she felt he was utterly emotionally unavailable. After much agonising, she decided to leave him. This decision brought with it a spiritual as well as a family and professional crisis. She broke away from her synagogue, stopped following religious rituals, and liberated herself from the orthodox dress code. Her family were horrified and put huge pressure on her to take her husband back. She felt lonely and isolated and at times suicidal. But, with the help of supportive friends from the liberal

Jewish tradition, she was able to forge a new relationship with her God, continued to pray and felt that she had developed a much more personal relationship with her deity.

Both psychoanalysis and Abrahamic religions embody broad-brush developmental models of the life cycle. Erikson and Erikson's (1998) 'stages' delineate the dilemmas we face at each point in our life journey—trust vs mistrust, identity vs role confusion, generativity vs stagnation, etc., each stage suggesting what can go wrong as well as right. The Kleinian model sees a never-fully overcome shifting equilibrium between paranoid–schizoid splitting and more wholistic depressive position thinking. Religion celebrates the seasons as well as the rites of passage of the life cycle—birth, adolescent sexual maturity, marriage, parenthood, maturity, decline, and death.

But the specificities of the 'spirit' with which we are concerned here never quite conform to pre-existing categories and way stations.

Elaine was a rather lonely little girl. Sent to an all-girls boarding school aged eight she found it hard to make friends or enjoy herself but had several 'crushes' on her fellow students. She dutifully went to church on Sundays, and as an adult conformed to the predetermined expectations of marriage, motherhood, and care work. The breakdown of her marriage triggered a religious as well as a personal crisis. She felt that she had never 'come clean' to God about her sexual love for other women. This led to her finding a more accepting and less dogmatic form of Christianity, where she began to flourish and in whose accepting arms she eventually became a respected elder.

In the face of uncertainty, religion is traditionally seen as a repository of 'eternal truths'. Likewise, Freud felt that his work illuminated the universality of the unconscious, of the oedipal situation, and the meaningfulness of dreams. But alongside this search for immutability, in both psychotherapy and spirituality there is a notion of a journey, a pilgrim's progress, a movement from darkness into light. The developmental processes illustrated by the examples suggest that within the human subject, our links to nature, and their interconnectedness, is an ever-shifting dynamic process. Both spirituality and psychotherapy can be seen as guardians of a process-informed perspective that contrasts with the a-historic, identity-driven discourse that prevails in much of contemporary life.

Conclusion

Based on in-depth interviews focusing on religious experience, I have drawn parallels with themes which also inform psychodynamic work. A sense of awe, transcendence of self-preoccupation and narcissism, the notion of a pilgrim's or psychoanalytic patient's progress on a developmental path, acknowledgement of mystery and unknowing, and a respect for the otherness of others and of the natural world, all these and more are to be found in both disciplines. Both spirituality and psychoanalysis attempt to find concepts and words to harness and so minimise the free energy integral to our being-in-the-world, while at the same time acknowledging the ultimate impossibility of this project. Enlightenment, sainthood, and fully analysed patient-hood remain unrealisable goals, but also hope-inspiring ideals.

CHAPTER 6

Jane Eyre as psychotherapist: torn between principle and desire

In this chapter we are squarely in the realm of the *aught*, but whose dilemmas arise unavoidably out of the *is*. In tackling the problems of what it might be to live a good life in a real world I'm suggesting that the solutions suggested by spirituality and psychotherapy correspond in ways that, were a dialogue between them to open up, could be mutually beneficial. This is because both are concerned with uncertainty and its consequences, and how living with this uncertainty—energy unbound—is intrinsic to our existence.

From a practical point of view, we, as individuals and collectively, are regularly faced with moral qualms. In major and minor ways we find ourselves daily challenged to work out what is the best thing to do in the specific circumstances which form the fabric of our lives. Should I buy these delicious-looking peaches wrapped in non-biodegradable plastic? Should I make a fuss about the fact that my husband seems to have forgotten our wedding anniversary? Should I drive to pick up the kids from school when we could just as easily walk? Should I take these antidepressants to lessen my misery, or will they blunt my feelings and render me zombie-like and ruin my sex life? Should I pay my builders in cash and so save money which I could then give to charity (or buy myself that new smartphone), when by doing so I am complicit in tax evasion?

Given that we cannot know the consequences of our actions, we depend on top-down Bayesian predictions or 'best guesses', often operating at a below consciousness level, to help us pick our way through these recurrent choices. If part of a religious culture, our moral outlook is usually propped up by preformed top-down precepts. Kant enjoins us to think for ourselves, but part of thinking for oneself entails listening carefully, but not in an enslaved way, to the wisdom of others. This then helps us to move from generalities to specific circumstances—thinking, and then acting, *judiciously*, as Neiman (2016) puts it, much as a judge knows her case law and precedents, but then applies them to the specifics of the cases brought before her.

Moral precepts can be thought of as portmanteau free energy minimisers in the face of uncertainty. Take the 'golden rule'—'*do unto others as you would have done to yourself*'. This, or a version of it, runs through most world religions. But easier said than done. Applying the golden rule in a judicious way depends on interpersonal skills relevant as much to psychotherapy as to spirituality. The rule highlights empathy, the ability to put oneself into another's shoes. This in turn depends on being able to tune in to one's own enteroceptions, and, again at a preconscious level, to imagine, feel, and rehearse with micro-muscle movements what the impact of our actions might feel like to another. (People whose facial muscles are paralysed by 'Botox' have been shown to be temporarily empathically compromised.) To do this, the rule requires us to stand outside ourselves sufficiently to be able to visualise the impact on others of our actions.

As we shall discuss in the next chapter, both other- and self-empathy are encompassed by the term 'mentalizing', the capacity to see others from the inside and oneself from the outside. Both too are predictive in the sense that they operate in the realm of uncertainty—there's no knowing for sure what the other may or may not be feeling. The golden rule is a spiritual value, a top-down instantiation of a precept that can help shape the incoherent jumble of bottom-up impulses that beset us when faced with the moral dilemmas integral to everyday living. Golden-rule-ism is also a skill that psychotherapy helps foster.

In medicine and the helping professions generally the version of the golden rule for practitioners runs '*first do no harm*'. In psychotherapy's case this means avoiding financial, informational, or sexual exploitation. But it's often difficult to tease out the rule as it applies to a specific case—especially when sifting short-term benefit from long-term maleficence. For therapists a minor version that I find helpful is: *when in doubt, stick to your boundaries*, however apparently helpful a short-run minor transgression might appear. A male therapist might ask himself, why not give this rather attractive female patient a hug? Maybe even a kiss on the cheek? And she looks as if she could do with a cup of coffee. She's asked for all three, she tells me she got precious few hugs as she was growing up, so surely it's going to help her to cheer her up and show her that life can be better than her miserable past—and isn't that what my job is supposed to be all about?

The 'slippery slope' to exploitation often starts in seemingly innocuous ways. Note that medicine's golden rule is framed in the negative—about not doing harm, rather than positively doing good. This is because negative free energy is more top-down predictable than its positive counterparts. Our taste buds are a thousand times more sensitive to bitter tastes than sweet ones, and likewise it is usually easier to see how to avoid being harmful than seeing a clear pathway to doing good. Indeed, in the selection and training of psychotherapy candidates, the main aim is to exclude those who are likely to do harm, rather than to find sure ways of choosing those who are going to do good.

In contrast to its parent discipline of medicine, psychotherapy can appear morally ambiguous. Therapist neutrality and non-judgemental validation might seem to evade a clear ethical stance. But behind this blanket of acceptance lie distinct moral principles. Mentalizing implies a detached and understanding view of one's own desires and putative actions, while at the same time seeing others as distinct autonomous agents deserving of respect rather than instruments to be used. Overall, a compassionate forgiveness of self and others (Gilbert, 2020) is intrinsic to the psychotherapeutic ethic. In the Kleinian canon, 'depressive position' thinking is favoured over splitting and projection: hatred, envy, and destructiveness are given their due, but seen as less mature and adaptive than their mitigation via conscious acknowledgement and the instantiation of a 'good internal object'. Psychotherapy works towards coherence and complexity, in place of chaos, denial, or starry eyed Pollyanna-ism.

Thus in most psychotherapeutic encounters there is an implicit ethical developmental edge in that one is trying to help clients move towards 'maturity'—away from the self-centredness of adolescence, towards enduring relationships and work projects, acceptance of both the opportunities and limitations of life, and some species of 'coming to terms' with these dichotomies. This is not far removed from normal caregiver fostered developmental scaffolding:

To take an everyday example. A three year old tries to hit his baby sibling. The parent might say something like 'No, X [using the child's name rapidly instantiates joint attention], we don't hit our baby brother. How would you feel if a big boy hit you?' Such admonitory 'deontic' communication helps the child to align his mental state with that of others (parent and the sibling) and to acquire the rudiments of mentalizing capacity. In a psychotherapy context that same individual might later discover that, starting with Cain and Abel, murderous feelings towards siblings are ubiquitous, and, ironically, that rather than condemning him to pariah-hood, having such feelings deepens his connections with fellow-human experience.

However, except in extreme cases such as child sexual abuse or violence, a therapist will always try to remain non-judgemental and morally neutral, aiming for understanding rather than the twin imposters of condemnation or praise. In contrast to ready-made spiritual or religious prescription, the aim is to hold on to uncertainty, working at the top end of the FEM hierarchy, helping the client to consider all options, to look at their dilemmas from all possible points of view, and to be guided in their actions by their 'gut' feelings, emanating not from superego prescriptions but what, bottom-up, 'feels right'. In this formulation, taking the totality of one's feelings into account is the strategy most likely to lead to 'right' action(s).

Thus in the case mentioned earlier where a deeply religious wife found herself profoundly unhappy in her marriage there was a painful battle between her allegiance to her top-down religious traditions and the family values which were so important to her, and her bottom-up life experience. Psychotherapy helped her to validate the latter and to negotiate within herself a way forward in which her values were not jettisoned, but renegotiated into a more complex formulation that enabled her to feel a degree of contentment and so better able to progress in her career and feel more loving and empowered in her role as a mother. The ethic of psychotherapy hinges on the hope that if the client can be helped to let the spirit of the unconscious speak through them, they will find a 'right way' to start to face, struggle with, and sometimes overcome the difficulties of their lives. By embracing uncertainty, chaos is paradoxically diminished, or if not, valued as a necessary cleansing preparation for new growth.

Let's illustrate this with an example, not from the consulting room, but from classic nineteenth-century English literature.

Jane Eyre, a penniless orphan, is employed by rich womanising landowner Mr Rochester, as governess to his ward Adele at Thornfield Hall. Unknown to Jane, Mr Rochester's mentally ill wife Bertha, a West Indian creole, is secretly confined in the attic of his mansion. After some initial verbal sparring, Jane and Rochester fall madly in love. It seems to be a good match—social class and age gap notwithstanding, they are equal fighting weight when it comes to wit and compatible worldviews.

Jane is no flirt, and finds it hard to think of herself as attractive to men. But despite, or perhaps because of, her traumatic childhood, she is a thoroughly thoughtful, mentalizing, self-motivated, independent-minded woman. Mr Rochester proposes to Jane. She happily accepts, unaware that she is being lured into bigamous transgression. Then, on the day of their marriage, as the banns are read at the church altar, Rochester's deception is revealed by his brother-in-law. Jane immediately and unequivocally rejects her suitor. He pulls male rank, eloquently pleading with her to go away to Europe with him, where none will be the wiser about his marriage to crazy Bertha. Although utterly distraught, and still madly enamoured of Rochester, Jane is steadfast in her refusal. This is what she says to herself:

The more solitary, the more friendless, the more unsustained I am, the more I will respect myself. I will keep the law given by God [i.e., one man, one wife]; sanctioned by man. I will hold to the principles received by me when I was sane not mad—as I am now. Laws and principles are not for times when there is no temptation: they are for moments such as this, when body and soul rise in mutiny against their rigour; stringent are they; inviolate they shall be. If at my individual

> convenience I might break them, what would be their worth?
> They have a worth—so have I always believed; and if I cannot
> believe it now, it is because I am insane—quite insane, with
> my veins running fire, and my heart beating faster than I can
> count its throbs. Preconceived opinions, foregone determi-
> nations, are all I have at this hour to stand by; there I plant
> my foot. (Brontë, 1847, p. 365)

Jane is Rochester's 'therapist', and her own, a wounded healer. She longs
to break boundaries, to run off with her man to sexual, intellectual,
and spiritual bliss and to explore the wider world, from which through
poverty and her gender she has been excluded. But she knows this is
'wrong', a violation not just of convention, but of the golden rule, her
Kantian categorical imperative. Because she can see beyond herself, is
able to access we-mode, in her heart she knows that, in the long run,
elopement could only be damaging to Bertha, herself, Rochester despite
his seductive protestations, and any future children they might have.

She sticks to her top-down principle which arises not out of superego-
ish rules, but deeply felt understanding of interpersonal pain. Anything
doesn't go. Rather than falling in with energy unbound, she does the
right thing, spiritually and therapeutically. This will precipitate a crisis for Mr Rochester, but eventually leads to a more complex binding
of his all-too-free energy. Bertha burns down Thornfield Hall and dies
in the fire. Trying to rescue her, Mr Rochester is blinded by a falling
rafter. But his wound leads to a profound healing. He is forced to face
his loss and emotional blindness. Jane reappears in his life. They are
now free to marry and have children, prompting Brontë's famous last
words—'reader I married him'. In this long haul, Rochester gains a 'borrowed brain' (and body!) in the shape of Jane. With both come the FEM
and spiritual maturation he has hitherto evaded. Jane's indomitable
spirit guides him into the ethically calm waters of loss, remorse, and
redemption.

Discussion

Implicit in both spiritual approaches and psychotherapy is the idea
of a 'good life'. 'Good' here has a dual connotation. A 'good life' can
be thought of as one that is satisfying, generates contentment and/or

happiness, is meaningful, and free from major psychological conflict or mental illness. But a good life is also an ethically good one—true to the golden rule, avoids inflicting harm on others or oneself, is unselfish, generous, and loving.

While both religion and psychotherapeutics have an idea of a 'good life', there is a subtle yet vital difference. In religious ethics there are clear top-down guiding precepts towards which we are enjoined to aspire. This for Jane was 'one man, one wife'. By contrast, psychotherapy's precept does not tell us what we should do or not do, but what we need to know—that is, ourselves. If Jane were to take her dilemma—'shall I dump the man I love, or elope with him illegally?'—to a therapist, the latter might respond roughly as follows:

> Let's think about the implications and background to each of those options. If you were to leave him, that would be a repetition of the many losses you have already endured: the deaths of both your parents, your kind uncle Mr Reed, and of your school-friend Helen. But were you to go down this path, the loss this time would be your choice and under your control. Perhaps you would be in a position fully to grieve the loss and move on, knowing that you have the power to love and be loved. On the other hand, despite your misgivings, were you to agree to Mr Rochester's offer, you would be embracing excitement and possibility and kicking over the traces of poverty and low self-esteem which have hitherto so constrained you. You would have to pay a price in the shape of permanent exile, but perhaps love would conquer all.

In the FEM model, ethical choices, good or bad, emerge from two types of 'conversation'—in the terms set out in Chapter 2, one Fristonian, one Winnicottian. First, in the interplay between bottom-up, incoming information about the world and the options it affords, and the pre-formed top-down precepts employed to bind them. Second in interpersonal transitional space, between the individual and their significant others, extending from intimates and family, through to cultural and group affiliations including those provided by religion. The latter provides a series of general ethical 'commandments', aperçus, precepts, and prescriptions backed up with caveats and threats of punishment for failing to adhere to them. Psychotherapy helps bring these general principles to bear on an individual life and series of choices, so that a 'judicious' pathway, in Neiman's (2016) term, can be chosen.

As in a psychotherapy session, a 'great' novel creates a transitional we-zone in which we can identify with its characters and see our own lives mirrored in them. Why does Jane so prudishly reject Rochester, we ask ourselves. Does she really need God to tell her what to do? But the application of the golden rule helps us to see the interpersonal consequences of our unregulated desire, and consider, even from a twenty-first century position of 'disenchantment', that Jane might be making the 'right' choice. Immersing ourselves in her experience adds to the store of top-down narratives we can draw on as we confront similar conflicts and dilemmas in our own lives.

In a secular context the psychotherapist shoulders a number of ethical responsibilities. Like Jane, who remains steadfast to her principles, she needs, in Bion's phrase, to be able to 'think under fire' and hold firm to boundaries, however beset by countertransferential chaos. At the same time she needs to be able to listen to these feelings, find ways to articulate them, and apply them to the specificity of the session and of the client's real-life dilemmas. And hovering above these practical skills, she will be guided by the ethic of self-knowledge, the need to bring disparate parts of the self into a coherent whole, and to foster skillful mentalizing. Which brings us to our next chapter.

CHAPTER 7

Attachment, mentalizing, and spirituality

Jane Eyre is an ethical mentalizer. She can read Mr Rochester's, Bertha's, and her own minds, see their differing points of view, and predict future directions, good, and not so good. This chapter looks at how the concept of mentalizing (Allen & Fonagy, 2006) can be applied to the secular spirituality integral to the psychoanalytic project. I shall argue that both mature religion and mature secularism, in contrast to fundamentalism, are consistent with a mentalizing perspective.

Jung (1968) saw psychoanalysis as a species of 'alchemy' in which the base metal of neurosis is transformed into psychic gold. 'Spirits' (volatile substances of low molecular weight) arise out of 'distillation'—releasing an essence through the application of heat. If the 'sublime' and the spiritual have a metaphorical poteen in common, Freud's definition of 'sublimation' is also relevant: 'A certain kind of modification of the aim and a change of object, in which our social valuation is taken into account, is described by us as "sublimation"' (1933a, p. 97); or if we prefer Shakespeare's *Tempest*: 'suffer a sea change/into something rich and strange'.

Freud saw a therapeutic aim as transforming symptomatic repressed affect into positive, socially useful, or aesthetically pleasing creative enterprises—the distillation of instinct into spirit. For Lakoff and

Johnson (1999), psychological states relate to body-orientation. Spirits, and heaven itself, are almost always pictured as high in the vertical plane. A patient troubled by outbursts of unbridled aggression, who begins to express his feelings through paint or song or dance, is moving in this sublimatory direction. He is becoming more 'spiritual' in the sense of being uplifted rather than brought low.

The 'spiritual' from this perspective has two key features: pro-sociality and relationality. In the heat of the therapeutic relationship, the holding and thoughtful affect co-regulation of the caregiver distils unbridled and potentially illness-generating feelings into construc-tiveness and connection. Seen from a free energy perspective, spiri-tuality is not a transformation of base drives into higher thought or 'intellectuality' as Freud saw it. Spirituality rather arises out of states of mind—cognitive and affective—that bring together top-down values with bottom-up impulses, and so helps people live with and to an extent transcend pervasive uncertainty. I shall argue that the concept of men-talizing represents a comparable psychoanalytic theorem.

A strong proponent of the sublimatory uplift perspective is George Vaillant (2008), well-known for his longitudinal studies of subjects from early adulthood through to old age (Vaillant, 1993). While his findings are generally consistent with the psychoanalytic emphasis on relation-ship as key to psychological health, Vaillant is critical of the compara-tive neglect of positive emotions in the psychoanalytic literature. He claims that positive emotions tend to have other-directed 'not-me', 'I–Thou' qualities, in contrast to the self-preoccupation intrinsic to the negative emotions on which psychoanalytic theorising tends to dwell. With his Alcoholics Anonymous-influenced invocation of the benign 'higher power', in contrast to the addictive and weak ego, he emphasises how most major religions foster the positive emotions of love, awe, for-giveness, compassion, and gratitude.

Vaillant's critique of classical psychoanalysis has to some extent been overtaken by the 'relational turn' (e.g. Mitchell, 1993) in psychoanalysis. The therapeutic role of loving affect is gradually coming to be acknowledged in the psychoanalytic literature (e.g. Akhtar, 2009; Music, 2014). A touching example comes from an interview with the Buddhist nun and novelist Jakucho Setouchi, as she reminisced about her analysis with Kosawa Heisaku (Harding, 2013):

> Every time he showed Setouchi to the door after an analysis, Kosawa paid her a compliment … On one occasion it was the pattern on her kimono; another time it was her coat. 'He never commented on my looks, though,' she says with a chuckle. It was all part of the treatment: an unprecedented unburdening followed by the last-minute lift of a well-directed kind word. Nothing like either of these things was on offer anywhere else in her life.
>
> 'To someone who's suffering, the importance of that just can't be exaggerated … When people come to me for help now, I listen to them and at the end I always find some little thing to compliment them on … When people are suffering … or when they're lonely, they need someone to notice them, simply to recognise them.'

Kosawa's compliments might be seen in some psychoanalytic quarters as seductive and transgressive of the neutrality rule. Nevertheless, drawing on the idea of defences against mental pain, psychodynamic thinking will look for a 'positive connotation' of apparently negative or symptomatic features. Depression might be formulated as attempting to mask unbridled rage, or repression as a way of avoiding the unbearability of childhood trauma.

Vaillant suggests that 'spirituality' can be seen as a cluster of positive and pro-social affective and relational phenomena built in to our nervous system via the limbic system and the right prefrontal cortex. For him the pro-social emotions—altruism and caregiving—have evolutionary survival value and are intrinsically 'spiritual'.

Attractive though it is, Vaillant's angle on spirituality is problematic. It is questionable whether his labelling of positive emotions and their psychological underpinning as 'spiritual' provides any added value. If 'spiritual' is synonymous with 'good' unselfish emotions, do we really need the term, unless its purpose is polemical, and even, ironically, self-serving, in that it reaches out to a constituency (the religious community) traditionally hostile to depth psychology? His contention that 'spirituality' is a good thing may turn out to be little more than a cuddly tautology. Vaillant elides a moral perspective—equating spirituality with seemingly value-neutral neuroscience—thereby providing a spurious justification for what is essentially an ethical/moral position, admirable though that may be. (Although, admittedly, a similar charge might be laid against the free energy minimising perspective I am here advocating.)

Attachment theory and spirituality

The roots of attachment theory lie in Darwinian evolutionary biology (Bowlby, 1990). Two general propositions underpin the evolutionary significance of the ubiquity of religion in human societies.

First, social groups in which altruism predominates over selfishness tend to have advantages compared with groups in which 'freeloading' and egotism prevail (Boehm, 2012; Wilson, 2019). In most ecologies, social cohesion and collaboration enable groups, and the individuals who comprise them, to overcome more successfully the challenges of existence—foraging, reproduction, child-rearing, and survival. However, as Freud well knew, alongside more positive features, depending on their ecological challenges and contexts, humans are also egotistical, narcissistic, and nepotistic (Haidt, 2012). The down-side to the cohesion-promoting virtues of religion is that with them come out-group antagonism, dehumanisation, and murderousness.

The task facing today's religious leaders is to foster cohesion while counteracting this out-group antagonism. Given that within the individual psyche altruism and unselfishness are comparatively weak forces, religion provides a vital external reinforcer and promoter of positive emotions, a necessary counterbalance to selfishness and devil-take-the-hindmost cultures.

A second point flows from the very fragility of life itself. Attachment theory posits the caregiver/care-seeker relationship as the fundamental basis for security, the psychological analogue of the immune system (Holmes, 2001). But given the unpredictability of both environments and social relationships, the capacity of caregivers, however altruistic, to protect their loved ones from death and destruction is at best limited; at worst, as in disorganised attachment, they may unwittingly be the very source of that lethal liability. This is where the afterlife aspects of spirituality come in, providing an ultimate top-down model with which to bind the free energy of death-awareness. In the Abrahamic religions God is invoked as universal protector, a bulwark against the inevitable and inescapable facts of loss and human destructiveness. Comparably, even in non-deistic Buddhism, the indestructible spirit is eternal, merely inhabiting earthly bodies as a temporary residence.

What's wrong with death is not death itself, since, at least in secular definition, it equates to the cessation of experience. But for social animals the problem of death is its concomitant loss, actual and anticipated—loss of one's loved ones, and, sooner or later, one's own existence, to which, unsurprisingly, one tends to be somewhat attached! To be alone and abandoned is, at least from an infant's perspective, equivalent to death. Hence Winnicott's (1962) famous, and often misquoted aphorism that 'there is no such thing as a baby ... A baby cannot exist alone, but is essentially part of a relationship.' Wherever one is in one's life cycle, a child-like sense of deathful isolation is likely to be triggered at moments of major loss. Suicide and deliberate self-harm can be seen as attempts to forestall, exert some control over, and bind the free energy associated with the unpredictability of inevitable demise.

God's role is to help ease the passage through bereavement, grief, and the accompanying emotions of anxiety, depression, and despair with far more assurance than is possible for imperfect human caregivers. As I've argued, since negotiating separation and loss is a central theme in attachment, a deity can be usefully viewed as an attachment figure, with a vital role to play in the dialectic of loving and losing that is the figured bass of all human life.

Ironically, those most in need of God (those with suboptimal childhood parental relationships) may have least access to him/her when needed, just as (and perhaps relatedly) those who most need oxytocin as a pro-social promoter (i.e. those with personality disorders) are those least likely to benefit from it when administered externally (Van IJzendoorn & Bakermans-Kranenburg, 2012). Nevertheless, sudden 'Pauline' conversion experiences which feature prominently in the Christian religious tradition can lead to permanent change in attachment disposition from insecure to secure ('earned security', Pearson et al., 1994), just as change in attachment status can be triggered in children when favourable circumstances (e.g. a single mother finds a loving new relationship) supervene (Murray & Andrews, 2005).

How 'psychological' is 'spirituality'?

Granqvist's attachment approach to religion outlined earlier could be described as 'instrumental' or 'functionalist'. It represents an example of the 'religion is good for you' perspective that, however empirically valid, provides a questionable justification for adding a 'spiritual' component to healthcare. Its weakness rests on the assumption that the undoubted benefits of belief flow causally, albeit mysteriously, from God him/herself, rather than the psychological constellation of which our conception of 'God' is a reified symbol.

The former Anglican Archbishop Rowan Williams (2012) is critical of such approaches. He argues that what he calls 'functionalism' is essentially secular, that is, pertaining to, and bringing benefits in the non-spiritual world, representing a kind of spiritual consumerism. He points out the irony of a fundamentalist religiosity which banishes uncertainty. By adhering to dogmatism, and so in a sense de-mystifying God, the very essence of spirituality is confounded.

> Secularism ... a functional, instrumentalist perspective, suspicious and uncomfortable about *inaccessible dimensions*—is the hidden mainspring of certain kinds of modern religiousness. (Williams, 2012, p. 15, italics added)

Williams's invocation of 'inaccessible dimensions' touches on the unbound energy which I suggest pervades the transitional zone where psychotherapy, spirituality, and religion overlap.

This takes us to the attachment-derived concept of mentalizing, or mind-mindedness (Meins, 1997), a psychological and relational construct which has uncertainty and unknowing built in to its being. The notion of mentalizing grew out of the phrase 'reflexive function', originally formulated as a subscale on the Adult Attachment Interview (AAI) (Allen & Fonagy, 2006; Allen et al., 2008; Main et al., 1985). Mentalizing can be defined as a subject's capacity 'to see oneself from the outside and others from the inside' (Holmes, 2010). The mentalizing perspective includes the following propositions: accepting that one's perception of the world is inevitably filtered through the mind; that it is therefore subject to error; that one can therefore never fully know another person's mind; that there are always different versions of reality, or narratives, depending on a person's perspective and context.

Uncertainty is thus thoroughly baked into the mentalizing approach. This is tempered by the idea that the better one mentalizes, the better able one will be to relate to and recruit others into 'we-mode' (borrowed brains and duets for one), and thereby to reduce uncertainty. In transitional space, the processes of dialogue, exploration, disagreement, and reconciliation, verbal and non-verbal, lead as a conversation progresses to a 'fusion of horizons' (Gadamer, 2013) in which people come to feel empathically linked, one with another, and with the disparate parts of themselves.

The mentalizing perspective acknowledges that another person's inner world can never be fully transparent. An exception to this, at least at an experiential level, is the state of being in love—whether this is mother–baby love or adult romantic/sexual love. But, equally, love, especially if infatuative, is notoriously blind, transient, and inherently somewhat delusional.

Dennett (2007) argues that this inescapable opacity is bypassed in two situations other than being in love. First, in drama and fiction, as discussed in the previous chapter, where the omniscient author, and vicariously the reader, are privy to the inner world of the story's characters. Second, in a person's relationship to a deity, who is conceived as being able to see directly into our hearts. To these I would add the psychoanalytic relationship, where the analysand is encouraged to observe and verbalise anything and everything that passes through his or her mind, in ways that do not and cannot occur in everyday communication, however intimate.

Mentalizing is a developmental achievement, not fully formed in infants and small children, but gradually gathering pace in the course of childhood and adolescence, and typically inactivated in states of extreme anxiety and various states of psychological disturbance. Fonagy et al. (2002) identify three 'non-mentalizing modes' which precede mentalizing developmentally, and may persist into adult life.

'Teleological thinking' entails an 'if this, then that' viewpoint which bypasses minds. No provisionality, no transitional space, no aught, just is. Teleology is a psychology based on actions and behaviours and end-games (hence its name), rather as pre-cognitive revolution behaviourism saw animal and human behaviour, up to and including language, in terms of stimulus, response, and reward. A teleological theology might entail the 'thought' (in inverted commas because strictly speaking thoughts do not exist in this mode): 'if I go regularly to Church, and give to the poor, my loved ones and I will be safe because God will look after us'. Compare: 'if my wrists are cut, then help will happen'—rather than the mentalizing thought: 'I am feeling really distressed and awful; I need someone to help me understand and soothe my distress'.

In *Hamlet* the agency-inhabited hero comes upon his hated uncle at prayer, vacillates over whether to stab him there and then, and justifies his indecision by reasoning, teleologically, that to kill him now would mean directly dispatching him to heaven: praying equals salvation irrespective of content or meaning of the prayer. But, following Dennett's (2007) formulation, we the audience have access to Claudius's inner thoughts in ways that Hamlet, his co-participant in the drama, cannot. Once Hamlet has left the scene, Claudius reveals, in mentalizing mode: 'My words fly up, my thoughts remain below: / Words without thought never to Heaven go' (*Hamlet*, Act 3, scene 3, line 113). Had Hamlet been able to mind-read/mentalize, and overcome his indecision, an awful lot of subsequent bloodshed might have been avoided!

In *'equivalence mode'* a person makes no distinction between thought and reality, one just 'knows' something to be the case, irrespective of evidence, or the 'triangulation' (cf. Holmes, 2010) that comes from secure interpersonal connectedness with its paradoxical acceptance of uncertainty. Here we are in the realm of pure aught, non-is. Freud's (1919h) 'omnipotence of thoughts' would be an example of equivalence mode. Similarly, the fundamentalist conception of scripture as the direct emanation of God is an equivalence analogue. To the extent that sacred text is seen as merely divinely-*inspired*, however, it is mentalized, since it is subject to question, clarification, and error. When Job (Chapter 19), immortalised in Handel's *Messiah*, says: '*If* it is true that I have gone astray ... I know that my redeemer liveth, and at the last he will take his stand upon the earth' (italics added).

The mentalizing signifier is the conditional 'If it is true that …', with which Job acknowledges the perspectival nature of his conviction. In equivalence mode no such contextualising qualifier would be evident.

In *'pretend mode'* the subject retreats into or fails to emerge from an inner world of fantasy in which the dialectic between thinking and reality is abolished and the external world viewed as illusory. Many religious phenomena—miracles and mystical experiences—could be seen in terms of pretend mode.

Differentiating 'primitive' non-mentalizing states from sophisticated mentalizing is not always easy. The Buddhist notion of impermanence, which holds that the 'true' nature of reality is an endless cycle of formation and dissolution, might seem, in the face of the apparent solidity of things and people, to be an example of 'pretend mode'. But given what we now know of geological and evolutionary time, of subatomic physics, and the failure of neuroscience failure to find a stable locus for the self among ever-changing brain states, the impermanence worldview may well correspond better with objective reality than our everyday working illusions of solidity and stability.

In the light of this classification of pre-mentalizing states, let's return to Williams (2012):

> The non-secular [i.e. spiritual] is, foundationally, a willingness to see things or other persons as *the objects of another sensibility than my own*, perhaps also another sensibility than our own, whoever "we" are, even if the "we" is humanity itself … What I am aware of, I am aware of as in significant dimensions not defined by my awareness. (p. 13, italics added)

For Williams spirituality entails recognising a viewpoint outside the self. This could encompass Williams's God, Kant's noumenon, Spinoza's panentheism, Buddhism's emptiness, or the mathematical truths to which science strives, but which because of the limitations of the human mind, it can never fully achieve.

Williams here resorts to a negative, defining 'non-secularity', or spirituality, as a decentring, an acceptance that there are 'more things in heaven and earth' than one's egocentrism would allow. This is his version of Keats's (2009, p. 277) famous letter to his brother about Shakespeare's genius: 'Negative capability, that is when man is capable of being in uncertainties, Mysteries, doubts without any irritable reaching after fact and reason'.

For Williams, spirituality is 'a field of *possible readings*, never therefore reducible to an instrumental account' (2012, p. 14, italics added).

This is consistent with the notion of mentalizing as a species of humility and awe in which one is constantly aware of the limitations and constraints of the mind, and how one's preconceptions and unconscious desires distort and shape experiences and relationships.

I'm arguing that both psychological and spiritual health are associated with radical provisionality. Under the aegis of a relationship with a therapist or in a religious context, transitional space is created where wishfulness and reality are prised sufficiently apart for new formations to arise. This is supported by the finding (Allen & Fonagy, 2006) that the capacity to mentalize is associated with favourable developmental experiences which lead one to trust that terrors will be soothed, errors corrected, distress alleviated, and hope enhanced—all in the context of a secure child–caregiver relationship. Given this, it comes as no surprise that the securely attached have a steadier, more benign, and accessible relationship to the deity, compared with the sudden lurches in and out of faith typical of the insecurely attached.

A digression about the normative implications of attachment terminology is now needed. 'Insecure' and 'secure' attachment refer to reproducible, validated, observable patterns of caregiver/care-seeker behaviours, predictive of whether or not an individual will develop psychological difficulties (Slade & Holmes, 2014). The delineation of contrasting positive, suboptimal, or pre-pathological epigenetic pathways marks attachment theory out from standard psychoanalytic thinking where the distinction between normality and pathology is sometimes hard to discern. However, a problematic aspect is that the terms themselves are value-laden. Few would cheerfully describe themselves as insecurely attached, even though such a classification applies to around 35% of a normal non-clinical population (Slade & Holmes, 2014). Indeed, from an evolutionary point of view, insecure attachment may well be an appropriate adaptation to the specific ecological conditions— often sub-optimal or worse—in which a child finds herself (Belsky et al., 2007). For example, if a caregiver is stressed, depressed, and irritable, it is adaptive, for the sake of a modicum of security and maintaining proximity, to suppress emotion and adopt an avoidant insecure pattern of relating to one's self and others. This may apply at a transgenerational level to populations that have been systematically exploited, oppressed, or marginalised. Parents who treat their children with a degree of rough neglect may be preparing them for survival in a similarly brutal world which they will likely later face. This exemplifies the 'positive connotation' of the phrase 'insecure attachment'.

The benefits of non-psychotherapeutic spirituality

Contrast this with psychotherapy's focus on enhancing mentalizing (Levy et al. 2006). Therapy typically (often unthinkingly) emphasises 'middle class' values: deferment of gratification; the capacity to articulate one's emotional and perceptual responses to situations and relationships; interpersonal sensitivity; realising the extent to which one's mind (as opposed to external adversity) makes one the author of one's own destiny, for good or ill. Psychotherapy tries to help people move from pre-mentalizing modes to these more mentalizing positions.

But what if mentalizing in specific circumstances is a bane rather than a boon? Too much thinking can make one vulnerable when action and self-protection, not reflection, is called for. Powerful emotions drive out mentalizing (Allen & Fonagy, 2006), whether these be negative—fear and anger and despair—or positive—states of arousal and intense love, sexual or parental. Teleological thinking ('I believe, so all will be well'), equivalence mode ('I *know* that God is on my side'), pretend mode ('my guardian angel will protect me') all work to keep hope alive and despair at bay. It would be unhelpful for these beliefs to be mentalized away as 'just thoughts', subject to error and as products of adverse developmental experience. Love of God may need to be unquestioning and absolute if it is to work its magic.

In addition, in the absence of a 'theory of mind', some species of spirituality provide their own route to comfort and survival, despite (or perhaps because of) being anti-psychotherapeutic. Challenging absolute beliefs may undermine their capacity to maintain hope and a sense of being part of a supportive community. An example of this is to be found in the popular spiritual guide, *The Power of Now* (Tolle, 1999). Tolle draws on Buddhist ideas in his exhortation to:

> free yourself from enslavement to the mind, enter into this enlightened state of consciousness and sustain it in everyday life. (p. 5)

> For him, all mental pain is a form of 'false consciousness': 'the unhappy and deeply fearful self … is ultimately a fiction of the mind', while enlightenment is 'not only the end of suffering and of continuous conflict within and without, but also the end of the dreadful enslavement to incessant thinking'. (p. 12)

There is clearly huge consolation in the idea that suffering can be eliminated in this way—by an acceptance of one's 'true self' which exists only in the present moment, unfettered by the ghosts of past pain and anticipated future fears. Tolle celebrates the deeper self, the 'no mind' (comparable to Bion's 'O') that lies beyond the thinking self, the self that transcends suffering and worry. He encourages one to 'get in touch with' this ultimate self as an antidote to mental pain. From a mentalizing point of view this could be seen as anti-psychotherapeutic in that it reinforces denial, and promotes evacuation of rather than transformation of painful thought and feelings.

Psychotherapy by contrast tries to help people to *experience* previously warded off sadness, depression, anger, and anxiety, so that that they can be contained, co-regulated, and learned from. Jung (1985), straddling both psychoanalysis and spirituality, helpfully deals with this dilemma with his aphorism that a necessary precursor to Buddhistic losing the self—is to find it. For him the job of psychotherapy would be to help with this preparatory stage before true 'no self' spirituality can be achieved.

There is much current interest in the role of mindfulness as an adjunct to psychotherapy (Safran, 2003). Mindfulness-based cognitive behaviour therapy (MBCBT) is an evidence-based treatment for a number of disorders including recurrent depression (Kuyken et al., 2010). The meditator is encouraged to observe thoughts—often negative and depressive ones—arising in him- or herself, but to view them as 'just thoughts' which can be peaceably relinquished. To the extent that the content and meaning of the depressive thoughts are discounted, as in Tolle's schema, this practice, however beneficial, could also be seen as 'anti-psychotherapeutic'. On the other hand, to see that a horrible intrusive thought is 'just a thought' is a mentalizing move in that it encourages an objective, external, non-self-centred perspective, defusing negativity and providing a degree of balm for the soul's suffering. In MBCBT the potential erroneousness of bottom-up experience is tested and challenged, while a top-down formulation of the mind as 'just a mind' similarly enables subjects to discount the veracity of their depressive thoughts and so, paradoxically, by binding their energy, loosens their grip on the mind.

Psychotherapy as spirituality

An important aspect of 'spirituality' is that it typically entails some sort of regular and often group-based praxis—prayer, confession, meditation, church attendance, chanting/singing, collective imbibing or smoking sacred substances, or ritualised movement and dance. Again typically, these activities take place under the aegis of an older/wiser, revered, endorsed initiate or leader.

Clearly there is a sense in which regular attendance at a psychotherapy session with a therapist, whether licensed or otherwise, for a fixed period ('the fifty minute hour') could be seen as a secular analogue of spiritual practice. Indeed, some explicitly make this comparison. In his interview with the author and neurologist the late Oliver Sacks, Higginbotham (2012) avers how:

> The relationship with his psychoanalyst, Leonard Shengold, a Manhattan-based Freudian specialist in child abuse and childhood trauma, is one of the most enduring in Sacks's life. In the dedication of *The Man Who Mistook His Wife for a Hat*, Sacks describes Shengold as his mentor; he has seen him twice a week almost every week for 45 years, and continues to do so. 'I saw him yesterday,' Sacks confirms, 'and I'll see him tomorrow.' [Sachs died in 2015.]

Alvi in Woody Allen's *Annie Hall* quips: 'I'm going to give my psychoanalyst one more year, and then I'm going to Lourdes.' I suspect Sacks's relationship with Shengold would by conventional psychotherapy research criteria be seen as 'supportive' rather than 'mutative', and the same is probably true of many long-term psychoanalytic relationships. As a psychiatrist, socialised to think in terms of time-limited 'interventions', I would have found myself somewhat disapproving of the idea of indefinite spiritualised therapy. It blurs the boundary between 'God' and Caesar which Jesus, when asked if Jews should pay their taxes to Rome, famously demarcated with the use of a coin (Matthew 22).

But the 'only mum will do' attachment relationship has continuity and specificity built into it. And the God/Caesar boundary is not so easy to separate. Coins have a third neutral 'side', albeit a narrow and unstable one, in addition to their two seemingly opposing 'faces'. Psychotherapeutic work might be seen as entailing a comparable balancing act. To mix the metaphor, psychotherapy has one foot in the world of symptom-alleviating Mammon, but the other firmly in that of the ongoing therapeutic relationship with its spiritual overtones.

Freud's version of Jesus's coin metaphor was his famous claim that 'much will be gained if we succeed in transforming … hysterical misery into common unhappiness' (Freud & Breuer, 1895d, p. 206), implying that analysis can take one so far and no further in understanding alleviating the pain of existence. Nevertheless psychotherapy can be an entry point into the world of spirituality, where 'common unhappiness' can be collaboratively considered, played with, transformed, and, in an increasingly secular world, offers a degree of rare comfort and consolation.

Enhanced 'spirituality' as a psychotherapy outcome

Psychotherapy's aim is 'mutative'—to produce change. The idea of religious conversion, particularly in its more dramatic or damascene manifestations, similarly implies a before-and-after state in which spirituality intervenes in a person's life to rescue them from despair and set them on a right road. In both, the assumption is that the mutative moment(s) will permeate the personality, affecting not just what happens in the consulting room or place of worship, but will generalise to transform a person's attitudes, relationships, and way of life.

This 'generalisation' means that, post-epiphany, the person will experience *enhanced connectedness*: to hitherto denied or neglected aspects of the self; to other people, and especially in intimate relationships; but also to society, nature, and perhaps even to the universe.

Despite disappointment, rage, revenge, and the need to retaliate, while life prevails, continuity outweighs loss. While there is life there's hope, if only in the tautological sense that without free energy minimising, life comes to a stop, at which point thermodynamics' second law takes over, as we move metaphorically from microorganism to ink drop.

'Connectedness' and continuity can be seen as spiritual narratives that provide a bridge, however fragile, over loss and neglect.

> Naomi was nearing the end of twelve years of once weekly therapy which she had sought hoping to overcome a number of 'borderline' features—substance abuse, self-harm, isolation, outbursts of uncontrollable rage, episodes of overwhelming anxiety. She was reviewing what had, and had not, changed in her life. She still felt unstable and lonely, and, albeit at reduced frequency, still resorted to self-soothing via substance abuse. But she now had a part-time job, a boyfriend, a dog, an allotment, a new house, and felt a degree of connection to her neighbours and small group of friends. She was furious at her therapist for imposing an ending, and wanted to walk out without a by-your-leave, but was, with prompting, able to tolerate her sadness and justified anger, turning her feeling of abandonment into a narrative with which she could live. Rather than out-of-sight-out-of-mind obliteration and revenge, she painfully acknowledged that her therapist could stay alive within her and that the spirit of what she had gained could, at least to some extent endure. Despite her disappointment and loneliness, she felt she was now unlikely to destroy the good things she had achieved in therapy.

The bridge building—however rickety—that were marks of Naomi's partial recovery resulted from a number of processes that perhaps therapy alone could provide. In the transitional space of therapy she could confront the chaotic free energy of her life rather than close it down with drugs or degradation. This was made possible by the borrowed brain of the therapist, who allowed himself unflinchingly to enter into her entropic world. On the basis of the virtual rehearsal provided by therapy she could begin to reach out to others and the natural world (including her dog) within the specific ecology of her hard lived life-niche.

Summary

In this chapter I've tried to develop an attachment perspective on the theme of spirituality and psychotherapy. I've suggested that Williams's advocacy of a non-dogmatic, non-instrumental approach to religion is consistent with a mentalizing approach in which ironic acceptance of uncertainty and error go hand-in-hand with the search for truth. I've conceded that pre-mentalizing formations—teleological thinking, equivalence, and pretend mode—characterise many forms of religion and provide top-down rubrics able—to an extent—to bind free energy, mitigate death anxiety, and provide guidance for living. But this comes at a price. Pre-mentalizing entails repression of the multitude of sensations and voices that make up lived experience, while clinging to unmodified shibboleths. Similar hazards attend psychotherapy itself, which can become a form of religion, deficient in the very self-reflexion it aims to foster in its clients. The search for false certainties, driven by the need for FEM, is an affliction far from confined to religion and spirituality.

CHAPTER 8

Tolstoy and secular spirituality

One aim of this book is to develop a landscape of 'secular spirituality' and its contribution to psychoanalytic work, resonant even for those like myself who describe themselves as 'agnostic atheists'. Agnostic atheism could be seen as a variant of 'Pascal's wager' (Jordan, 2007), and is inherently mentalizing in that it subjects one's own views to the scepticism of uncertainty.

I have already placed my cards—or card—on the table and suggested that a key measure of change in psychotherapy is *enhanced connectedness*: to oneself, in the sense that hitherto denied or neglected aspects of the self, however painful, are given voice; to other people, and especially in one's intimate relationships; but also to society, nature, and ultimately to the universe. 'Connectedness', I argue, brings with it a deepened sense of meaning in a person's life. This 'meaning' is a species of spirituality in that it is not in itself material (although of course composed of material objects—including fellow humans) but is a manifestation of the *patterns of relationships* between people and their environment, human and non-human. From the free energy perspective, pattern implies information and thus is anti-entropic.

We've had help from Charlotte Brontë. My next example comes from Tolstoy's *War and Peace* (1869). I have chosen it partly because Tolstoy was in his lifetime and beyond a spiritual, albeit idiosyncratic, leader, influencing among others, Gandhi and Martin Luther King. He was implacably opposed to orthodox religion, while being equally insistent in his advocacy—although not always their praxis in his own life—of the spiritual values of humility, chastity, equality, non-violence, and reverence for what he called 'the infinite'.

The passage I have chosen illustrates recovery from a withdrawn depressive state, but also the wider connectedness implicit in secular spirituality. It illustrates movement from depressive pseudo-certainty into the transitional zone of hope. Its context is the 'holding' provided by novelistic form (a flexible yet bounded structure comparable to that of the consulting room or place of worship) and the guiding but non-controlling authorial voice. Part of Tolstoy's greatness as a novelist is his ability to stand back and let his characters feel, fail, explore, discover for themselves. The psychotherapy parallel speaks for itself.

The sequence comes at the beginning of 'Part 3'. Prince Andrei is a rich, handsome man in his early thirties, intelligent and capable, but bored and disillusioned, embodying some aspects of Tolstoy himself prior to his marriage to the much younger Sophia. He could easily be a psychoanalytic patient in present-day Hampstead or Manhattan.

Andrei is doubly bereaved. His mother is dead, and he shares his household with his sister and domineering father. His wife—whom he did not love—has recently died in childbirth, leaving him with a young son.

It is early spring. Andrei is making a journey to inspect one of his many estates. Here is the famous 'oak tree' passage.

> At the edge of the road stood an oak ... It was an enormous tree, double a man's span, with ancient scars where branches had long ago been lopped off and bark stripped away. With huge ungainly limbs sprawling unsymmetrically, with gnarled hands and fingers, it stood, an aged monster, angry and scornful, among the smiling birch trees. This oak alone refused to yield to the season's spell, spurning both spring and sunshine.

'Spring, and love, and happiness!' this oak seemed to say. 'Are you not weary of the same stupid meaningless tale? ... I have no faith in your hopes and illusions' ... there were flowers and grass under the oak too, but it stood among them scowling, rigid, misshapen and grim as ever.

'Yes, the oak is right, a thousand times right,' mused Prince Andrei. 'Others—the young—may be caught anew by this delusion but we know what life is—our life is finished!'. (p. 492)

Prince Andrei is required by aristocratic protocol to stay the night with a local grandee, Count Rostov. As he approaches the Rostov mansion he catches sight of a young girl, Natasha Rostov: pretty, playful, laughing, carefree.

'... that slim pretty girl did not know or care to know of his existence ... What is she thinking of? Why is she so happy?' Prince Andrei asked himself with instinctive curiosity. (p. 493)

In his room after dinner Prince Andrei throws open his window, and eavesdrops on Natasha and her cousin Sonia eulogising the balmy summer's evening:

Two girlish voices broke into a snatch of a song ...

'Oh it's exquisite! Well, now let's say good night and go to sleep.'

'Sonya Sonya! ... Oh, how can you sleep? Just look how lovely it is! Oh how glorious! Do wake up Sonya!' and there were almost tears in the voice. 'There never, never was such an exquisite night .... I feel like squatting down on my heels, putting my arms round my knees like this tight—as tight as can be—and flying away! Like this ...'

'And for her I might as well not exist!' thought Prince Andrei ... for some reason hoping yet dreading she might say something about him ...

All at once such an unexpected turmoil of youthful thoughts and hopes, contrary to the whole tenor of his life, surged up in his heart ... (p. 495)

Prince Andrei leaves early the next morning. Later, on his way home he catches sight of the old oak. It is a wonderful day:

> Everything was in blossom, the nightingales trilled and car-olled, now near, now far away ... The old oak, quite transfigured, spread out a canopy of dark sappy green, and seemed to swoon and sway in the rays of the evening sun. There was nothing to be seen now of knotted fingers and scars, or old doubts and sorrows. Through the rough century-old bark, even where there were no twigs, leaves had sprouted, so juicy, so young it was hard to believe that aged veteran had born them.
>
> 'Yes it is the same oak,' thought Prince Andrei, and all once he was seized by an irrational, spring-like feeling of joy and renewal ...
>
> 'No, life is not over at thirty-one,' Prince Andrei decided all at once, finally and irrevocably. 'It is not enough for me to know what I have in me—everyone must know it too ... that young girl who wanted to fly away into the sky ... all of them must learn to know me, in order that my life not be lived for myself alone ...'

One reading of this passage would see it as a description of recovery from grief and mourning—the gnarled oak tree, with its lopped-off branches representing the isolation and withdrawn-ness of loss; its bur-geoning forth next day a mark of renewal and hope and the overcoming of despair and bereavement. The transformation is triggered by Prince Andrei's fleeting encounter with Natasha, his feeling the first flickers of new love.

The oak tree and the rising sap of spring here would be no more than a 'pathetic fallacy' in which neutral events in nature are used sentimen-tally and therefore 'fallaciously' (according to Ruskin, the coiner of the phrase) to illustrate human emotions.

From a 'spiritual' point of view, however, the passage can be read rather differently. Prince Andrei, partly through his mother-deprived and father-dominated upbringing, partly through bereavement, partly due to his intrinsic character—arrogant, self-centred, cynical—is in a disconnected, emotionally avoidant state, spurning the spring life that teems around him. Then, through his 'instinctive curiosity', the exploratory vector that in its full form arises out of secure attachment, he encounters the innocent girl on the brink of adulthood. Just as she reaches out to the spring night, so he finds himself reaching out beyond himself to her. This self-extension is a first step away from his egocentric self-absorption. He glimpses that there is another centre of existence, independent of and as yet indifferent to himself.

This very indifference is a 'narcissistic blow', a burst of unminimised free energy. But because it is *contained* (within his room, by the beauty of the night, within the compass of the novel and its author) it stimulates him to mentalize. He begins to see himself from the outside, and the other (Natasha) from the inside. He experiences desire—to be connected—for the girl, but also to nature. He longs and 'decides' to 'swoon and sway', to leave his 'knotted fingers and scars' behind.

The pattern that connects is not merely arbitrary—a 'fallacy'—but a psycho-spiritual reality. Man is part of nature, and the 'green fuse' (Thomas, 1957) that drives the oak tree is the same biological force that (re)awakens in him hope and desire, love and compassion. Natasha's self-hugging can be seen as an adolescent first step towards sexual relatedness, but the libido or life-force (with its hormonal and neurological underpinnings) is consonant with the energetic processes captured by the notion of 'spring'—sappy green leaves, carolling nightingales, smiling birch trees. Andrei's metamorphosis is therefore not merely metaphorical. There is a pervasive pattern running through him to and from the nature to which he opens himself. This is his 'spiritual' awakening.

Love is a form of everyday therapy. Andrei, if he is to 'succeed' in his advances towards Natasha, will have to cope with the possibility of rejection. His encounter with Natasha reawakens the life-force within him, pushing him to risk the trade-off between the benefits of love and the dangers of rejection.

Comparably, psychotherapy can only take one so far. There comes a point—a point of both liberation and trepidation—where one has to leave the security of one's therapist and her consulting room and venture into the wider world. If therapy is successful, the beneficiary will, with the help of the therapist's borrowed brain, have negotiated the free energy of transitional space. Psychotherapy patients have, we therapists hope, been sufficiently strengthened by the rupture/repair cycles of therapy to be able better to take risks. Our aim is to help them forge a new set of top-down values and principles with which to navigate the highs and lows, the rapids and rocky setbacks of everyday life.

The oak tree passage illustrates two central ethical values common to psychotherapy and spirituality. Both entail movement or process: the movement from isolation to relatedness, and from non-mentalizing egocentricity to empathy with the other, and oneself. Implicit in the latter is the aforementioned 'golden rule' of reciprocity—do unto others as one would have them do unto oneself. The 'spiritual' case I have argued in relation to the oak tree story suggests that the golden rule is not merely a covert form of self-interest—the selfish gene knowing which side its bread is buttered, although it can be that too. Implicit in my reading of Tolstoy's story is the view that at a fundamental level the other *is* oneself. I and thou are made from the same stuff, with the same desires, hopes, fears, vulnerabilities, and ambitions. In our we-mode we are part of the continuity of nature that stretches beyond the merely human. In his discussion of Levinas's concept of compassion and the inescapable 'face of the other', Black (2023) makes a similar point.

Another link between spirituality and psychotherapy is contained in the attitude each takes towards suffering. Prince Andrei is clearly unhappy—albeit in the typically avoidant pattern of deadened feelings—but the idealised tone of Tolstoy's writing means that a full acknowledgement of the experience and transcendence of psychic pain is postponed. It is only later in the novel, when Prince Andrei is mortally injured fighting in the Napoleonic War that he begins to feel his pain, and this is only possible because he is nursed through his terminal illness by Natasha and can draw on her 'borrowed brain'. Only then can the extent of his Christ-like existential 'wound' and suffering unto death become explicit.

In his excoriating critique of bland post-Christian platitudes offered by neo-religious apologists such as de Botton (2012) and Spufford (2013), Roman Catholic turned Marxist Eagleton (2014, p. 206) reminds us that Christian faith: 'is not about moral uplift, political unity or aesthetic charm ... Nor does it start from portentous vagueness of some "infinite responsibility". It starts from a crucified body.'

As Vaillant (2008) rightly notes, psychoanalytic literature focuses more on negative than positive emotions. But contra-Vaillant, this is surely entirely appropriate: alleviating mental pain is the primary rationale for psychoanalytic therapy. The *context* is always one of hope and trust, but the *work* entails the identification, experiencing, naming, and co-regulation of negative affect. A typical psychotherapy session might start with the patient feeling 'bad' in some way. The therapist enters into the maelstrom of this misery, and may herself become temporarily infected and affected by it. Now it is the therapist who feels useless, incompetent, all at sea. Staying with those feelings, seeing them as grist to the therapeutic mill, representing an aspect of the patient's inner world—feelings too painful perhaps for the patient to have faced on his or her own—patient and therapist (like Natasha as she holds dying Andre's hand) then together work to encompass them in a framework of mutual understanding. With luck—and not a little skill—by the end of the session there will be a lightening-up, a sense of a movement, glimmers of hope and even pleasure, of a job done, hand-to-mutual-hand, collaboratively.

Implicit in seemingly value-neutral psychotherapeutic ethics is the principle that facing mental pain, rather than sequestering it or overlaying it with false hope and reassurance, is the true route to transformation. But it is a facing—and 'facing up'—that is done collaboratively with the therapist. A similar ethic is central to the Christian notion of sacrifice. Christ suffers with and for us, and thereby our burden is lightened. The psycho-biological roots of this empathic suffering lie in the co-regulation of affect that is a central part of the parental role, which when performed sensitively and responsively, forms the foundation for secure attachment (Slade & Holmes, 2014).

In Buddhism too, suffering stands centre-stage. Prince Gautama's confrontation with poverty, disease, and death led him to abandon his golden-boy protected existence and seek enlightenment and a simple life. Buddhism embraces the paradox that the first step towards release from suffering is acceptance that to suffer is inevitable and unavoidable. Suffering here links with the notion of 'impermanence'. Everything—living and non-living—is subject to change. Our conception of fixed entities, including mental pain itself, is illusory. This idea is vital for therapists, especially when working with extreme states of mental pain, particularly suicidal feelings and impulses. The justification, and basis for hope, is the conviction that however awful one feels at any given moment, impermanence will ensure that today's suicidal feelings will look different in tomorrow's light.

CHAPTER 9

Spiritualised psychotherapy

My challenge in this penultimate chapter is, by recapitulation, to persuade readers that bringing a 'spiritual' dimension into psychotherapy practice is no fey add-on but practical, relevant, and quotidian.

In this task I am guided by a number of overarching principles. The first is *the sacrosanctity of the therapeutic space*. Ironically, the parameters of a consulting room, while in the terms of my argument embodying secular spirituality, are mundane, banal even. A typical consulting room is likely to be neutral in décor, comfortably but unobtrusively furnished, free from interruptions, smartphones, temperature extremes, or loud noises. These bourgeois parameters convey an important albeit ambiguous signal. The client is given the message that this is a safe space, while at the same time one that is sufficiently unoccupied to accommodate and absorb her chaotic preoccupations, embarrassing thoughts, stories, dreams, and phantasies, and to allow them to expand and, *pace* Taylor (2007), establish a temporary sense of *fullness*. (A former psychoanalytic colleague and friend provided wonderful therapy for people whom, quoting Fanon, she dubbed 'the wretched of the earth'. She maintained that she didn't mind where she saw her clients—an ill-lit windowless broom cupboard would do if that was all the NHS could provide.) When this sense of safety cannot be maintained—as it was for a Jewish colleague working with an Islamic patient at the height of the Gaza crisis of 2023—where the consulting room is invaded by the outside world, then therapy must temporarily be paused.

A parallel here is with a Protestant place of worship, especially those free from graven images, gold-leafed icons, tinkling bells, or wafting incense. A simple Zen Buddhist sanctuary might convey a similar message. Notwithstanding, Freud's consulting room was bedecked with antiquities proclaiming his belief in the archaeology of the psyche, while present-day analysts are not above iconising their founder's portrait on their walls, while their bookcases silently legitimize the theories underpinning their arcane working methods.

The second principle flows from the fact that the therapeutic space is a shared one. Therapist and patient are in this together. Like respectful priest (Fairbrother in George Eliot's *Middlemarch*, for instance) and parishioner, although their roles differ, there is a sense of *shared-brain equality before the workings of the unconscious*. The therapeutic relationship is democratic and equal, albeit in a 'lopsided' way (cf. Barratt, 2012).

A third and vital principle is *the primacy of the unconscious*. Dreams, daydreams, free associations, and fleeting thoughts articulate the language of the psyche, unsullied by guile, pretence, or therapeutic zeal, as encapsulated in Rycroft's (1996) evocative title *The Innocence of Dreams*. The unconscious does not provide an objective account of external reality. For that to emerge, as I have suggested, a playful 'transitional space' shared-brain encounter between top-down inner worlds and bottom-up sensations is required. The 'soul-work' of the psyche provides the vital clues or 'material' which needs to be listened to, verbalised, and reconnected with by therapist and client together. In parallel with the client's self-exploration, the analyst attends to her own unconscious for clues about the client's inner world. In a comparable way, perhaps, religious people listen to the 'voice of God' as a guide, a sign, and pointer to emotional truths.

Another, and somewhat paradoxical, quasi-spiritual aspect of therapy is encapsulated by Bion's (1970) famous injunction to the analyst to enter the session—'without memory or desire'. This can be reformulated as *unprejudiced receptiveness*, comparable to the Zen concept of 'child mind' or the 'emptiness of emptiness' (Thich Nhat Hanh, 2011), or in the Christian tradition, *kenosis* or self-emptying (Sorenson, 2004). Therapeutic *kenosis* includes emptying oneself of 'helpfulness' in the form of suggestions, advice, prescription, or the desire to make decisive interpretations. Consciously, both patient and therapist want the suffering soul to get better from whatever conflict or misery besets them. But too strident therapeutic efforts to help may be experienced as manipulative or coercive. The therapist's job is to be in control *of* the setting—place, time, frequency, ending and beginning of sessions, etc.—but never *controlling* of what goes on in it. A mutual participatory space is created; beyond that there is no predetermined agenda. Anything can happen—good, bad, dull, exciting, stimulating, soporific. Yet within the psychoanalytic compass, nothing never happens.

This 'empty' receptiveness links to the principle of *ethical neutrality*. There may be a powerful desire on the part of the patient to cling on to their illness, not to change, to 'keep hold of nurse for fear of something worse', to perpetuate their dependency, to prove to themselves and, as they perceive him, their puffed-up therapist, that the world is an inhospitable and abusive place. Therapies that brush this negativity aside fail to help the patient learn from the deep and developmental truths of their negativity. Therapeutic space is ready for anything that 'comes up', however painful, unexpected, or seemingly destructive.

This can be compared with the Christian and Islamic tradition of confronting 'sin' and the Devil and their workings head-on, or the relentless Zen master's efforts to rid his students of play-acting and self-deception (Fromm, 1986). Given that, as Hamlet (Act 2, scene 2) reminds us 'there is nothing either good or bad but thinking makes it so', therapists try (with varying degrees of success) to unshackle themselves from both praise and condemnation, from over-eager or premature encouragement to replace id with ego, paranoid–schizoid thinking with depressive ditto, or insecure attachment with secure. A military principle is that time spent in reconnaissance is never time wasted. Being open to negativity and setting aside battle plans with which to tackle it is a vital part of the therapist's skill.

A final principle, and one which perhaps contradicts some of the above, is the non-negotiability and universality of *hope*. As Emily

Dickinson puts it: 'Hope is the thing with feathers / that perches in the soul … / I've heard it in the chilliest land / and on the strangest Sea …' (Hughes, 1968, p. 41). From a negentropic point of view, there are very few circumstances outside unbearably painful terminal illness in which it is better to be dead than alive.

The hope-imbued therapeutic stance is an embodiment of the conviction that the client's difficulties can, with help and time, be overcome, mitigated, or at least lived with. Hope is also central to spirituality, whether for forgiveness, the possibility of an afterlife, the eco-cyclical sense that 'this too will pass' (a Zoroastrian adage), or the Buddhist notion of impermanence and therefore the transience of suffering. As a therapist one is necessarily from time to time beset by hope's antithesis, despair—only too aware of the limitations of one's skills, and/or the entrenched-ness of one's clients' difficulties, especially when they overlap. For psychotherapists supervision is a vital ingredient of the hope-maintaining apparatus. This leads to the importance of supervision. To switch magisteria (Gould, 2002), even the pope has a confessor (Holmes & Storr, 2023). The more detached supervisor can take up the baton of hope and help struggling therapists (i.e. from time to time all of us) to see how malign doubts are co-created and to suggest how they might empathically reflect the client's traumatised inner world, rather than, or at least alongside, a realistic appraisal of one's own inadequacies.

I now segue, unavoidably, into autobiographical mode. Beyond technique, training, and supervision, each therapist and every therapy is sufficient unto itself, a manifestation of the myriad experiences, influences, and contexts, present and historical, that bear upon a present moment, co-created by two similarly dissimilar human beings. This uniqueness should not be underestimated, and pushes against simple methodologies for evaluating psychotherapy. Even identical twins—first born, second born, etc.—from the moment of birth have a different life-course, and inhabit a non-shared as well as shared environment. The therapist's task is to pull together the component elements that make up this complexity. Every session is in search of its bedrock truths, general statements that at the same time encompass the specificity of an individual life. This apple falls today out of this tree on my allotment, but Newton's generalisation from his own seventeenth-century experience describes perfectly (or, as Einstein would have it, nearly perfectly), half a millennium later, the speed, acceleration, trajectory, and impact of its fall.

What follows is an attempt to tease out some of the 'spiritual' aspects of one person's everyday clinical practice.

Each session starts before it begins. I enter the therapy room a few minutes in advance, settle myself in my chair, and aim to bring myself into the present moment by focusing, in a meditation-like way, on my breathing. My domestic and emotional concerns are temporarily set aside. I try to open my awareness to my surroundings, to attend to the sights, sounds, and smells of the room's ambiance. My aim is to make the familiar as unfamiliar as possible, as though I was experiencing it anew. None of this is quite as explicit or delineated as this description suggests; there is a routine here-we-go-again aspect. But I am in search of the 'freshness' of secure attachment and the mentalizing stance which that implies.

The doorbell rings, there is a knock, or I press 'admit' on my Zoom screen. The patient announces themself. An entrance has a spiritual, wholistic aspect. The person who comes into this therapeutic space brings their body, mind, and soul—not to mention handbag, vestments, mobile phone, and other accoutrements, or occasionally, as an Argentinian psychoanalyst once described to me at the height of the civil war in that country, as in *The Sopranos*, a gun. Much but not all of the physicality of this is lost in increasingly common post-Covid e-sessions. This loss is to an extent balanced by a glimpse of the patient's home setting—a 'room', an unmade bed, a strolling-by cat, a neat or not-so-neat sofa, a coffee cup comfortingly hugged.

There is a pause. Exhaled breath, a cloud of unknowing—a cartoon question mark hangs above us. In what direction will the therapeutic conversation go? Does it matter? *Il n'y a que le premier pas qui coute.* The important thing is to get going. Once we're under way we must trust that our unconscious, and the 'third' of the conversation itself will take care of the rest. A nudging starting gun may be needed: 'Mmm' or even a mere clearing of the therapeutic throat.

The client begins to speak. It could be anything—or 'nothing', a no thing that, spiritually speaking, is always a something. How she felt while travelling to the session: she had to change underground trains,

London's Circle line was closed. If on Zoom, how she was forced to move room to get away from workmen's noise. Or a family row story. Or, 'I don't know what to talk about.' 'My mind's gone blank.'

It's a squiggle (Winnicott, 1962), or chess game. The patient always plays white, makes the first move. Now it is my turn. I'll reflect and riposte. Probably it doesn't matter much what I say, more important is the tone of voice and rhythm, 'What does that [blank] feel like?', or 'Row? *Wow*' (contingency and marking).

But I'm pondering too, my thoughts coloured by the ubiquity of transference. Is it me that's the therapeutic workman? Do the noise of my thoughts and utterances block out hers? What is the direction of our therapeutic travel? Is there change in the offing or are we just going round in circles? Was there a suicide on the line, did they bring up her self-harm feelings? I'm listening to my unconscious: giving it free rein: a horse on the loose, associations are 'sove-reign'. I'm receiver as well as transmitter. I'm trying to decipher my unconsciousness's message. It may not be God's voice, but it comes from a no-self place, our 'third', our duet for one, our jointly created transitional space.

Multitasking, I'm listening to the patient too. What she says, but also what she's *not* saying. Some of what she's not saying she *is* saying, but in a song without words—a gesture, a clasping and unclasping of the hands, a tone of voice, a silent tear, a sweeping back of the hair, a change of posture, a cough, a rasp in the throat. Then there's the stuff she's not saying because she doesn't know it is there, or cannot bear to let it be there, or be seen to be there. Yet, in this co-inhabited transitional space—the unbound feeling/energy can't be got rid of, so it's I who must suffer it, bind it, name it. A pain strikes my chest—maybe the pain of loss unacknowledged. A welling up of my eyes. Could this be latent love? Now there's a fear this therapy business might get out of hand—sheer terror of madness, or death, or unbridled eroticism.

It's time for me to try to say something, preferably useful. Psychotherapy is ultimately a dialogue or its nothing. I try—not always successfully—to eschew *ex cathedra* therapist statements, but some sort of 'interpretation' is called for. Ah, the i-word. The analytic therapist's stock in trade. And what exactly is this thing called an 'interpretation'? Whence do they come? Most contemporary analysts would say that the starting point for an interpretation is the analyst's unconscious (Civitarese &

Ferro, 2022; Ogden, 2016), stimulated by the client's 'material', and therefore subsumed under the rubric of countertransference.

I think of the therapy session as a form of everyday creativity, like cooking a meal, going for a round-trip walk, repairing a broken cup—with its beginning, middle, and end 'product'—food on the table, a satisfying sense of having taken exercise, entropy temporarily reversed. We're halfway now, in the middle of our session's Dantean journey. I try to watch my thoughts as they arise and find a way to bring them into my conversational offering. I tend to hedge my comments around with qualifiers and hypotheticals: 'The thing that comes to mind for me is ...'; 'I could well be wrong but I wonder if ...'; 'Perhaps what we're talking about here is ...'; 'Let's imagine the real issue here is ...'

A young man who came into therapy after the break-up with his long-term girlfriend is describing his ritual 'addictions'—betting on horses, following the minute-by-minute fortunes of his shares on the stock market. 'My brain is hyperactive. It just won't stop buzzing away, telling me I shouldn't be doing all this, but the more it says that, the more I seem to carry on doing it. Me and my brain seem always to be at odds.'

He labels his obsessiveness as 'self-harming'. We discuss how the more he engages in theses 'addictions' the worse he feels and the worse he feels the more he engages in them.

This 'analysis' is not exactly new and certainly not showing him a way out from his self-generated mind-trap. Meanwhile, behind my listening, and at variance with the rational tone of our conversation I find myself feeling strangely sad and tearful. Drawing on this, I suggest that behind his rituals there's a lonely sadness which he is desperate to avoid.

Suddenly, and with held-back tears, he talks about the dog which he and his former girlfriend had in lieu of a child, and how sad he felt when, in the break-up, he lost both of them.

Later he brings up the 'dry rot' in his house and his uncertainty about how extensive the damage it has caused will be—will he need to rebuild the entire house?

I try to find a formula which brings together the session's themes, past, present, and transference. I grab the psychoanalytic notion of the 'combined parent', suggesting that, like his own separate-world parents, he and his brain, he and his ex-partner, and perhaps he and me if rebuilding his life is too big a task, can never quite find ourselves in the same place at the same time. 'Yes', he says, 'it's as though I am still waiting for my life to begin.'

I find myself ending the session by describing a poem by Sharon Olds (2005) in which a woman looks at a photograph of her parents in the first flush of youth and love just after they have met, and how she, wise after the event of a warring and abusive marriage, wants to say '*Just don't do it,*' but then realises she cannot *not* endorse their union, because without it she wouldn't exist.

This unashamed boundary-breaking freedom to bring myself and my reading into sessions seems to be a function of age and stage in my therapeutic life cycle. I suspect my younger self would have been horrified by this gratuitous intrusion. But *the spirit* moved me. I followed its dictation.

But what is this 'spirit'? If Dickens's *Christmas Carol* is to be believed, a spirit knows its *place*. It haunts locations. The spirit of therapy dwells in the interpersonal space between client and therapist, Winnicott's play space. An 'interpretation'—in the example of my proffering the 'combined parent' concept—is a ready-made construct available to be pushed to-and-fro by therapist and patient. Psychoanalytic theory is a storehouse of such playthings. It is the therapist's job to bring them to life, to deploy them creatively. Sometimes new ones need to be forged.

Doing therapy is more and more for me a kind of automatic writing. Mine not to question why. This too is an age-related aspect, beyond technique, akin to the therapeutic creativity which writers such as Bion (1990), Eigen (1998), Milner (1987), Ogden (2017), and Civitarese and Ferro (2022) champion.

And yes, the infinite potential of silence. A dwelling in the inner world, attending to the top-down and the endogenous bottom-up, bracketing off external intrusion. The therapist needs to know when just to let be—staying with her own inner thoughts and respecting the patient's need to be with theirs, while all the time waiting for something to 'come up' as it is often put—a nugget of truth, regurgitation of a trauma, or a mere burp.

The session progresses. A story, a shape, a narrative arc begins to emerge. I try to get a sense of what this session is 'about', and how that fits into the patient's overall life-trajectory. This is intrinsically a top-down imposition, an attempt to create order out of the messy chaos—free energy—of lived experience. Sometimes 'diagnosis' helps: tummy ache and fever, translate, under close scrutiny, via rebound tenderness in the right iliac fossa, into appendicitis and from there to appendicectomy. It all makes sense. Rising wages and roll back of aristocratic power in the Middle Ages become explicable once the impact of the Black Death is factored in, creating a labour shortage and therefore enhanced worker bargaining power vs the autocracy (Hickel, 2021).

Religion similarly provides a fund of moral stories, parables, and anecdotes into which an individual life with its highs and lows can be fitted: the fall of man, temptation, parricide, fratricide, selfishness vs altruism, forgiveness, redemption. Would that the psyche/spirit were so simple. Broad brush moral tales no longer suffice. With the rise of the individual, the specificity and mentalized perspectives of the 'story'—as depicted in art, poem, novel, film—take over from parable and passion play as objectifications of social and emotional life. In *Great Expectations*, Pip's journey from humble origins to empty respectability; the class-coloured ambivalence of his love for Estella and hers for him; the unredeemed trauma of Miss Haversham's jilting and the final meltdown conflagration of her frozen life.

Psychoanalysis provides a map of human psychological development centred on family life—'birth, copulation and death' as T. S. Eliot put it. In the session all this is brought to life via the mystery of transference. Transference is 'mysterious' because we find ourselves caught in its force field of energy unbound without consciously willing or wishing it.

Paul, a single man in his early forties, had left a trail of broken relationships behind him, and his current one was already in jeopardy. He brought a dream in which *he was at a railway station with his son, a nameless woman, and a cheetah. They were due to visit a friend in another part of town. They started walking but got lost. Roger thought they should call an 'Uber', but worried that he didn't know his friend's postcode and wasn't sure what the rules were about cheetahs in taxis.*

His first association to the dream was the classic Katherine Hepburn film *Bringing up Baby* where Cary Grant's only way to the heroine's heart was through her pet leopard.

There was a lot of 'cheating' in Paul's background story. As a child he would sometimes cheat to get better grades in exams in order to win his parents' praise; and he had felt that his mother 'cheated' on him when he was displaced by his sister as the pride-of-place top-dog child.

I mused aloud about envy of loving couples and then wondered if there was a theme of 'cheating' somewhere. Paul then described how all his relationships had come to an end when he had 'cheated' with another woman. Shamefacedly Paul then confessed that, unknown to his therapist, he had consulted a CBT practitioner hoping that she would provide a faster route to cure, rather than the slow walking pace of his existing therapy—he was looking for a taxi ride to health and therapist who was 'Uber'—that is, superior—to his psychoanalytic one.

Using a simple parent/adult/child formulation, I then speculated that parent and child modes were those most likely to lead to 'cheating'. The neglected child (Paul was sent to boarding school aged seven while his mother had experienced long periods of depression) was desperately in need of comfort wherever he could find it; any rebuff or interruption in an ongoing relationship would trigger seeking elsewhere. Equally, the parental role (which Paul often found or manoeuvred himself into with his partners) with its deontic prescriptions inevitably evoked rebellion and transgression—'why the hell *should* I toe the fidelity line?'. Only his adult self was in the position to weigh the options and uncertainties and work out a practical 'settled down' golden-rule course of action.

All this could be said to comprise the 'spirit'—the motive force—which had brought the dream into being. Driven by his ghosts in the nursery (Fraiberg et al., 1975) Paul brings his psychic DNA into the relationship with the therapist, lays his wounds out for inspection—offers his mental iliac fossa for palpation. The spirit of psychotherapy lay in the hope for a different outcome: to feel that, despite sibling rivalry, he still was lovable and loved; to hope that he could be accepted for what he was, rather than having to aggrandise himself with grade inflation; to acknowledge the pain and selfishness implicit in deceit and cheat, and to ask, via 'understanding', for forgiveness.

The end of the session looms. I have to draw a line in our sand play, to mark a boundary between the transitional space of the session, where spirit holds sway, and the realities of time, space, and person. But also, through 'holding in mind', to communicate that Paul and I will meet again and that my inner representation of him will carry us over the causeway of separation and loss. We shall be physically apart until the next session, but the *spirit* of therapy and the patient's presence, his pain and hopes, live on to play another day.

CHAPTER 10

Coda and credo

Like most psychotherapists, I tend to get asked to which branch of that broad church I belong. While unashamedly ecumenical, not to say maverick, my primary allegiance is to attachment theory with its roots in both relational psychoanalysis and science-based ethology. In this chapter I list some of the 'spiritual' values which provide a background context for my work as an attachment-oriented psychodynamic psychotherapist.

Trust the universe

In their magnificent final chapter of *Attachment in Adulthood*, Mikulincer and Shaver (2007) argue that secure attachment equips one to face the existential issues of death, unfettered freedom and the search for meaning with a degree of equanimity. Compared with their insecure counterparts, the securely attached are more autonomous, better able to endure separation, to feel comfortable with their identity, to accept imperfection and ambiguity, equipped to explore and tolerate the unknown, and, in the spirit of all these, to draw more easily on support and help:

> Secure people … can take a healthy leap of faith and commit
> themselves fully to their choices, and at the same time be open
> to the possibility that their decisions will be wrong. (Mikulincer
> & Shaver, 2007, p. 475)

Note the use of ecclesiastical language in this everyday context—'leap of faith' has escaped here from its religious confines.

Avoidant people tend to be beset by feelings of meaninglessness, as was Prince Andrei before his encounter with Natasha; conversely the ambivalently attached may pin their hopes on a single/simple truth or dogma. Secure attachment ensures faith in the ultimate meaningfulness of existence (inseparable from relatedness), the capacity to tolerate periods of confusion, and the need continually to update and readjust one's perspectives.

Whether consciously or unconsciously, psychotherapists often have little alternative other than to 'carry on carrying on' in the face of despair, and misery. We have to live with a sense of the limitations and inadequacy of what we have to offer. We trust that things will turn out all right, while knowing that sometimes this will be a false hope. Survival against odds is part of our evolutionary inheritance. Given the cosmic improbability of life—even at a microscopic unicellular level—it is not entirely delusional to believe that 'good' can triumph over doubts, anxieties, destructiveness, perversity, rejection, and abandonment. It is better to exist than not to exist. And, ironically, believing this to be so enhances its likelihood.

The ubiquity of suffering

As already described, as a therapist one has to be able to immerse oneself in one's patient's misery and pain. One must accept, like Shakespeare's dyer's hand (Shakespeare, sonnet 111), that one will inevitably be affected—stained even—by the nature of one's work. One will recognise too that one's own confusion and pain will have played their part as motivations for choosing to make this field one's life's work.

A highly literate but painfully depression-afflicted patient, infuriated by her view of me as embodying the 'division of suffering', in which she and her fellow patients feel the pain, while doctors, psychiatrists, and therapists stand by and smugly watch, puffing themselves up as the 'ones who know', barked out King Lear at me: *'Take physic pomp; expose oneself to feel what wretches feel.'*

At the same time, through contingent or earned security, the therapist holds on to faith in the capacity of people to survive, recover, and find hope; not to dwell in past guilt and shame or future fear and terror; but live with and in the present; to accept and mourn what cannot be altered; and find the agency, assertiveness, and legitimate anger to change that which is mutable.

Professional ethics

As therapists we are no more 'spiritually advanced', psychologically healthy, immune to suffering, no less cruel, selfish, and confused than our fellow humans. Indeed, we are often a lot more of all these than most. However, we hope that in the consulting room the very role we adopt, backed by training and experience, enables us temporarily to put ego and its flaws to one side and offer our better selves in the service of our patients. Like musicians, whose skill makes them a vehicle and vessel for composers' creativity, 'we' are a conduit through which the healing process and its spirituality can express itself. Ultimately, the 'interpretations' to which we give voice come from the depths of our being, realms beyond the purview and jurisdiction of the conscious and humanly flawed self.

Non-attachment

Sahdra and Shaver (2013) and others (e.g. Holmes, 1997; Safran, 2003) have noted the paradox in the linguistic discrepancy yet conceptual proximity between the Buddhist notion of 'non-attachment', and the attachment concept of secure attachment. In Buddhist theology 'non-attachment' might appear to denote what in attachment terms would be 'detachment', avoidance', or 'deactivation'—implying affective withdrawal from intimacy, a seeming self-sufficiency or splendid isolation.

But non-attachment can be viewed, rather, as the ability to occupy the middle ground, to take into account all possible perspectives, including the certainty that one will at times be wrong, to give one's hopes and desires and longings their due, without succumbing to blind pursuit of ever-elusive certainties. Non-attachment is above all an affirmation of the freshness and fluidity of life, a liberation from stasis and rigidity, and an immersion in the creative possibilities of transitional space where free energy and its binding vie for the upper hand. Non-attachment recognizes the limited sample of the universe which our senses provide. Top-down spirituality is able to acknowledge this, to know that there is so much we don't and can never know.

Attachment theory emphasises the seamless capacity of securely attached children to handle both attachment and separation, and as adults to accept loss as the coin-face of connection, and to adapt to the circumstances in which they find themselves without conformism or 'false self' function. A degree of avoidant detachment may be needed when faced with rebuff, and a measure of anxious clinging when inconsistency threatens, but the secure retain the ability to stay grounded, having an ultimate confidence in relationship and the dangers of isolation.

During a rather intense psychotherapy session in my outpatient office in the hospital where I worked as a psychiatrist, the door suddenly swung open, and a patient from the inpatient ward (whom I'd 'sectioned'—that is, detained against his will—on the previous day) burst in and shouted 'Dr Holmes you're an absolute bastard,' then slammed the door shut and disappeared. There was a stunned silence, or pregnant pause, until the patient piped up from the couch, 'Do you know, I believe that's what I've been wanting to tell you—but have never quite dared—for the past nine months.' As therapy progressed both she and I were grateful to that chaotic intrusion.

Disorganised attachment represents the ultimate in relational disruption and destructiveness. Yet the securely attached, as can the 'non-attached', know that 'disorganisation' is never far away. We live on the edge of chaos, of increasing entropy—socially, individually, biologically—yet refuse to despair or give up, or perversely to celebrate and augment chaos.

Freedom and necessity

A theme running through this book has been that the term 'spirituality' points to an implicit pattern connecting the psychological and the social, the human and the non-human, the organic and the non-organic.

Freud (1933a) proudly claimed that his discovery of the power of the unconscious and the converse limitations of the conscious mind, was, after Galileo and Darwin, the third of the great Enlightenment blows to man's narcissism. The relevance of this to psychotherapy is as a reminder of the extent to which are nested within the interlocking histories of our evolutionary past, the structure and function of our nervous systems, our historical place in the world, the vicissitudes of our own family narratives. People seek therapy because they want to 'change'. But, paradoxically, change comes about only to the extent that we can accept ourselves—and feel accepted—as we are (cf. Linehan et al., 2006). Our capacity to change our destiny depends on being able to accept our weakness, vulnerability, helplessness, our Freudian 'castratedness' (Barratt, 2012). Contra Rousseau, we are not born free, but find ourselves held everywhere within the chains of history.

A common thread for psychotherapeutic and spiritual perspectives is a 'thirdness'. Transitionality transcends the limitations of the self, beyond both the freedom of the imagination, and the necessities of history and biology. From this observing, self-reflective, oedipal, deontic, and deistic position we can see both poles and give due weight to both. Freud's triangle extends far beyond mother, father, and child, although it may originate there, into the existential essence of our being.

Seen thus, spiritually and psychotherapeutically, emotional freedom *is* possible. This 'third' is at home with paradox—securely attached parents can accept that their children love and hate them with equanimity. In a further parental paradox, freedom flows from the creative use of constraint. The boundaries of the family—and the consulting room—enable creativity to flourish. As Dylan Thomas's *Fern Hill* puts it:

> Time held me green and dying
> Though I sang in my chains like the sea

As therapists we try to bring into focus the constraints of which our patients' sufferings are a product, and therefore to learn to forgive; to live in a present moment imbued with spirit, and which is always relational—with the Other, with the natural world, and with ourselves. Psychotherapy helps us sing in our chains, to stay 'green'—ecologically and chronologically.

Conclusion

Coming from a position of agnostic atheism, this book has been informed by four basic principles. First, that the 'spiritual' cannot be thought of as a separate realm, beyond the bio-psychosocial perimeter of psychotherapeutic practice. Either nothing is sacred, or everything is. For a psychotherapist, no aspect of human life, however 'negative', is alien. Second, no consulting room is an island. Although relationships with fellow humans are primary, human psychology is part of a web of connections and patterns that extend into the non-human living world and the inanimate sphere of the material universe. Third, the fundamental process of which we are a part—energy, matter, time, evolution, creation and destruction—are lawful, whether these 'laws' are seen as sufficient unto themselves, or as 'pan-entheistic' (Davies, 2006) manifestations of an animating deity.

Finally, humans are blessed—and perhaps cursed—with the ability not just to suffer joy and misery, but also to reflect on those experiences. This self-reflexive, stepping-back faculty—the mentalizing vantage point—is itself a product of evolutionarily driven developmental processes. When things go well, caregivers' reflexivity enables them to pass on that capacity to their offspring; much of the work of psychotherapy is concerned with trying to re-establish that developmental track in people for whom it has gone awry. And it is in the jointly created transitional space between belief and brute fact—or 'brute beauty' as Hopkins's Windhover would have it—where free energy binding finesse happens.

Learning to mentalize can be thought of as 'spiritual' in two ways. The idea that a pristine truth is ultimately inaccessible is intrinsic to the idea of mentalizing. The error-prone, self-constrained mind can never fully apprehend the mysteries of the thing-in-itself. But one of psychotherapy's tasks is to help people move *towards* that reality, and the paradoxical freedom and ethical benefits it bestows. Mentalizing is also 'spiritual' in the sense that it implies a degree of non-attachment, the capacity to lean away from oneself and to view suffering—one's own and others'—with equanimity and compassion, as well as activating the steps needed to alleviate it. To conclude: from this attachment perspective, psychotherapy is no more, and no less, than an intensely practical and loving pathway to spiritual awakening, in a pressingly secular world.

CHAPTER 11

Summary

In the course of this brief book I have ranged—nay, skimmed—over a wide variety of topics and viewpoints. Below is my attempt to summarise the main points with which I have been wrestling.

1. We live in an age of 'disenchantment', where religious belief and practice can no longer be taken for granted.
2. In parallel with this, there has been an emptying out of inner life, and a sense of loss of meaning.
3. In the Western world identity is increasingly defined by consumerism, physical appearance, victim status, and digitised self-advertisement.
4. But this leads to an ontological insecurity which drives a hunger for spirituality, a realm beyond utilitarian exchange, which acknowledges what has been lost, and points to ways in which it can be recovered and valued.
5. The praxis of psychotherapy has the potential to fill this spiritual vacuum, offering an intense relationship that cannot fully be measured by its exchange value, which offers a geography of

the inner world, and which helps build a more organic sense of self-in-relation-to-others.

6. Psychotherapy views personhood as part of a wider matrix, 'horizontally' with the village of family and friends, and beyond that with the biosphere and physical environment, and 'vertically' as part of developmental and historical processes.

7. Nevertheless, the role of psychotherapy is Janus-faced. In its solution-focused 'wellness' guise it can reflect and reinforce the very social values of hyper-individualism that bring its clients for help. On the other hand, to the extent that it opens up an alternative social space untrammelled by instrumentalism, it challenges the prevailing culture.

8. Living creatures must negotiate a world of radical uncertainty in order to stay safe, survive, and reproduce. There are aspects of our lives, those of others, and the world in general which are unknown and unknowable, unpredicted and unpredictable.

9. Karl Friston's neuroscience model of FEM addresses this radical uncertainty in ways which correspond with the psychoanalytic idea of the need to 'bind' psychic energy (aka libido) as an antidote to entropic chaos.

10. In the FEM conceptualisation, the brain, bombarded with incoming 'bottom-up' information from the senses, external and internal, attempts to gives meaning to this, as best it can, by binding it with 'top-down' preformed models of the world. This binding is based on Bayesian predictions based on prior experience and novel constructions.

11. The role of spirituality and psychotherapy correspond in that both are cultural formations offering anti-entropic top-down free energy-binding models of the world.

12. They tackle radical uncertainty along two dimensions: a) by opening out a *transitional space* in which via relationship or 'borrowed brains', the free play of the imagination is liberated, and b) as a result, creating new and more *salient top-down models* with which to understand oneself and one's experience.

13. Radical uncertainty is especially significant for those suffering with psychological illness and whose developmental experiences have

often been chaotic and loss-ridden, and whose current lives often repeat these patterns.

14. Salutary parallels between secular spirituality and psychotherapy include: moving from self-centredness to non-ego states; being part of a group (which may be no more than the therapeutic relationship) larger than oneself; balancing egotism with altruism; trusting the unconscious; acknowledgement of the ultimate limitations of consciousness.

15. Religion's top-down energy-binding FEM precepts range from the generic and simplistic to complex and mystical. Psychotherapy brings a *self-reflective dimension* to FEM in which the thoughts and feelings with which we negotiate existential uncertainty are questioned and contextualised environmentally and developmentally.

16. In the secular spiritualised version of psychotherapy praxis advocated here, the therapist aims to cultivate non-ego states; to adopt a compassionate and reverential respect for the present moment; to acknowledge and encompass the client's environmental connections, human and ecological; to attend to their own and their client's bedrock existential experience; and to forge a self-reflective language and narrative that, paradoxically yet truthfully, is both definitive and partial.

Appendix

The aim of this qualitative study was to delineate the part played by religion in believers' lives, present and past. The interviewees included people from backgrounds of Islam, Anglican Christianity, Methodism, Unitarianism, Catholicism, Druidism, Wiki, Hindu, reform Judaism, and humanistic agnosticism. The sample was 'opportunistic', in that it was drawn from friends, family, recommendations, and acquaintances. It was, I believe, a representative sample of people from a variety of faith backgrounds.

The focus of the interviews was explicitly not on the details of a person's specific beliefs and their justifications. My aim was to understand 'lived religion'—its developmental history and how it helps or doesn't help with the tribulations of living, and how it shapes a person's routines, thoughts, and relationships.

Each interview consisted of roughly an hour-long tape-recorded conversation with the participant. Interview methods were essentially those of a psychotherapist. I tried to be as receptive, non-judgemental, curious, and respectful as possible. I confined my interventions to attempts to clarify or extend the participants' comments, and to summarise what I thought they were saying, so that they could modify, confirm, or disagree with my synopses. I guided the interview with a small number of semi-structured open-ended questions (see below). I took written notes during the interviews. These were then transcribed and I subjected them to qualitative analysis, looking for themes, common topics, especially those with psychotherapeutic relevance.

After an introductory section in which I explained the nature of the project and left time for interviewees to ask questions about the recording process, etc., I asked all respondents the same set of open-ended questions. All gave permission for their answers to be recorded and analysed, as long as they were anonymised.

The seven questions were as follows:

1. Can you say something about your upbringing and background from a religious and spiritual point of view?
2. What about adolescence and young adulthood? Did your religious or spiritual experiences and convictions change during that phase of your life?
3. What if anything does the term 'spirituality' mean to you?
4. Can you say something about the part which religion and spirituality play in your everyday life today?
5. Do religion and spirituality play any part in maintaining or regaining good mental health and equilibrium? Have there been difficult periods or moments in your life when you have turned to religion or spirituality?
6. What does the term 'sacred' mean for you, and how does it relate to our discussion so far?
   Brief pause/break
7. Have we left out any important themes or issues, and can we talk about them?

Qualitative analysis identified a number of overarching themes discussed in Chapter 6: attachment and comfort in times of trouble; narrative and a sense of meaning; the existence and importance of an inner world; developmental perspectives and the spiritual life cycle; right action; awe and transcendence; belonging; ritual and routine.

References

Abed, R., & St John-Smith, P. (2022). *Evolutionary Psychiatry.* London: Royal College of Psychiatrists.

Akhtar, S. (Ed.) (2009). *Good Feelings: Psychoanalytic Reflections on Positive Attitudes and Emotions.* London: Karnac.

Allen, J. (2022). *Trusting in Psychotherapy.* Washington, DC: American Psychiatric Publishing.

Allen, J., & Fonagy, P. (Eds.) (2006). *Handbook of Mentalization-based Treatment.* Chichester, UK: Wiley.

Allen, J., Fonagy, P., & Bateman, A. (2008). *Mentalizing in Clinical Practice.* Washington, DC: American Psychiatric Publishing.

Aviv, R. (2022). *Strangers to Ourselves.* London: Penguin.

Ayer, A. (2000). God-talk is evidently nonsense. In: B. Davies (Ed.), *Philosophy of Religion.* Oxford: Oxford University Press.

Ballatt, J., Campling, P., & Maloney, C. (2020). *Intelligent Kindness* (2nd edn.). Cambridge: Cambridge University Press.

Barratt, B. (2012). *What Is Psychoanalysis?* London: Routledge.

Barrett, L. (2018). *How Emotions Are Made.* London: Penguin.

Bateman, A. W. (2022). Mentalization-based treatment. In: S. K. Huprich (Ed.), *Personality Disorders and Pathology: Integrating Clinical Assessment and Practice in the DSM-5 and ICD-11 Era* (pp. 237–258). Washington, DC: American Psychological Association. https://doi.org/10.1037/0000310-011.

Beck, A. (1975). *Cognitive Therapy and the Emotional Disorders*. Maddison, CT: International Universities Press.

Belsky, J., Bakermans-Kranenburg, M. J., & Van IJzendoorn, M. H. (2007). For better *and* for worse: Differential susceptibility to environmental influences. *Current Directions in Psychological Science, 16*(6): 300–304.

Benjamin, J. (2017). *Beyond Doer and Done to*. London: Routledge.

Bion, W. R. (1967). *Second Thoughts*. London: Heineman.

Bion, W. R. (1970). *Attention and Interpretation*. London: Tavistock.

Bion, W. R. (1990). *Brazilian Lectures*. London: Karnac.

Black, D. (Ed.) (2006). *Psychoanalysis and Religion in the 21st Century: Competitors or Collaborators?* Hove, UK: Routledge.

Black, D. (2023). *Psychoanalysis and Ethics: The Necessity of Perspective*. Hove, UK: Routledge.

Blass, R. (2023). The puzzle of Freud's puzzle analogy. In: L. Brown (Ed.), *On Freud's Moses and Monotheism* (pp. 126–142). London: Routledge.

Boehm, C. (2012). *Moral Origins: The Evolution of Virtue, Altruism and Shame*. New York: Basic Books.

Bollas, C. (2019). The democratic state of mind. In: D. Morgan (Ed.), *The Unconscious in Social and Political Life* (pp. 27–38). London: Phoenix.

Bowlby, J. (1971). *Attachment*. London: Penguin.

Bowlby, J. (1990). *Charles Darwin: A New Biography*. London: Hutchinson.

Britton, R. (2015). *Between Mind and Brain*. London: Routledge.

Brontë, C. (1847). *Jane Eyre*. Penguin Classics. London: Penguin, 2006.

Brown, G., & Harris, T. (1978). *The Social Origins of Depression*. London: Tavistock.

Cahart-Harris, R., & Friston, K. (2019). REBUS and the anarchic brain: Toward a unified model of the brain action of psychedelics. *Pharmacological Reviews*, July, *71*(3): 316–344. DOI: https://doi.org/10.1124/pr.118.017160.

Civitarese, G., & Ferro, A. (2022). *Playing and Vitality in Psychoanalysis*. London: Routledge.

Coan, J. A. (2016). Toward a neuroscience of attachment. In: J. Cassidy & P. Shaver (Eds.), *Handbook of Attachment* (3rd edn.) (pp. 242–269). New York: Guilford.

Coan, J. A., Schaefer, H. S., & Davidson, R. J. (2006). Lending a hand: Social regulation of the neural response to threat. *Psychological Science, 17*(12): 1032–1039.

Damasio, A. (2004). *Looking for Spinoza*. London: Vintage.

Davies, P. (2006). The physics of downward causation. In: P. Clayton & P. Davies (Eds.), *The Re-emergence of Emergence: The Emergentist Hypothesis from Science to Religion*. Oxford, Oxford University Press.

Dawkins, R. (2008). *The God Delusion*. Boston, MA: Houghton Mifflin.

De Botton, A. (2012). *Religion for Atheists*. London: Hamish Hamilton.

Dennett, D. C. (2007). *Breaking the Spell: Religion as a Natural Phenomenon*. London: Allen Lane.

Donne, J. (2006). *Selected Poems*. London: Penguin Classics.

Dunbar, R. I. M. (2022). *How Religion Evolved: And Why It Endures*. New York: Oxford University Press.

Eagleton, T. (2009). *Reason, Faith and Revolution*. New Haven, CT: Yale University Press.

Eagleton, T. (2014). *Culture and the Death of God*. New Haven, CT: Yale University Press.

Edelman, G. (1992). *Bright Air, Brilliant Fire: On the Matter of the Mind*. New York: Basic Books.

Eigen, M. (1998). *The Psychoanalytic Mystic*. London: Free Association.

Elder, A. (2023). Personal communication.

Epstein, G. (2006). *Psychotherapy as Religion*. Reno, NV: University of Nevada Press.

Erikson, E., & Erikson, J. (1998). *The Life Cycle Completed*. New York: W. W. Norton.

Feldman, R. (2015). The adaptive human parental brain. Implications for children's social development. *Trends in Neuroscience*, 38: 372–399.

Ferenczi, S. (1928). The elasticity of psychoanalytic technique. In: M. Balint (Ed.), *Final Contributions to the Problems and Method of Psychoanalysis* (pp. 87–102). New York: Brunner/Mazel, 1980.

Field, N. (2005). *Ten Lectures on Psychotherapy and Spirituality*. London: Karnac.

Fonagy, P., & Allison, E. (2014). The role of mentalizing and epistemic trust in psychotherapeutic relationships. *Psychotherapy*, 51: 372–380.

Fonagy, P., Gergely, G., Jurist, E., & Target, M. (2002). *Affect Regulation, Mentalization, and the Development of the Self*. New York: Other Press.

Fonagy, P., Rost, F., Carlyle, J.-A., McPherson, S., Thomas, R., Pasco-Fearon, R. M., Goldberg, D., & Taylor, D. (2015). Pragmatic randomized controlled trial of long-term psychodynamic psychotherapy for treatment resistant depression: The Tavistock Adult Depression Study (TADS). *World Psychiatry*, 14: 512–521.

Fraiberg, S., Adelson, E., & Shapiro, V. (1975). Ghosts in the nursery: a psychoanalytic approach to the problems of impaired mother-child relationships. *Journal of the American Academy of Child Psychiatry*, *14*: 387–421.

Freud, S. (1900a). *The Interpretation of Dreams. S. E., 5.* London: Hogarth.

Freud, S. (1907b). Obsessive actions and religious practices. *S. E., 9*: 115–128. London: Hogarth.

Freud, S. (1919h). The 'Uncanny'. *S. E., 17*: 217–256. London: Hogarth.

Freud, S. (1933a). *New Introductory Lectures on Psycho-Analysis. S. E., 22.* London: Hogarth.

Freud, S. (1939a). *Moses and Monotheism. S. E., 23*: 3–137. London: Hogarth.

Freud, S., & Breuer, J. (1895d). *Studies on Hysteria. S. E., 2.* London: Hogarth.

Friston, K. (2010). The free energy principle: A unified brain theory? *Nature Reviews Neuroscience, 11*: 127–138.

Friston, K., Fortier, M., & Friedman, D. A. (2018). Of woodlice and men: A Bayesian account of cognition, life and consciousness. An interview with Karl Friston. *ALIUS Bulletin, 2*: 17–43.

Friston, K., & Frith, C. (2015). A duet for one. *Consciousness and Cognition.* http://dx.doi.org/10.1016/j.cogn.2014.12.003

Fromm, E. (1973). *The Anatomy of Human Destructiveness.* London: Penguin, 1997.

Fromm, E. (1986). *Psychoanalysis and Zen Buddhism.* London: Unwin.

Gabbard, G., & Lester, E. (1996). *Boundaries and Boundary Violations in Psychoanalysis.* New York: Analytic Press.

Gadamer, G. (2013). *Truth and Method.* J. Weinscheimer (Trans.). London: Bloomsbury.

Garland, C. (2018). Group-analysis: Taking the non-problem seriously. In: *Foundations of Group Analysis for the Twenty-first Century: Foundations.* Abingdon, UK: Routledge.

Gergely, G., & Watson, J. (1996). The social-biofeedback model of infant parenting. *International Journal of Psychoanalysis, 77*: 1181–1197.

Gibson, J. (1986). *Ecological Approaches to Visual Perception.* Hillsdale, NJ: Laurence Erlbaum.

Gilbert, P. (2020). Compassion: From its evolution to a psychotherapy. *Frontiers in Psychology, 11.* https://doi.org/10.3389/fpsyg.2020.586161.

Gilligan, C. (2011). *Join the Resistance.* London: Verso.

Gleik, J. (2004). *Isaac Newton.* London: Penguin.

Gould, S. (2002). *Rocks of Ages: Science and Religion in the Fullness of Life*. New York: Ballantine.

Granqvist, P. (2006). On the relation between secular and divine relationships: An emerging attachment perspective and a critique of the 'depth' approaches. *International Journal for the Psychology of Religion, 16*: 1–18.

Granqvist, P. (2020). *Attachment in Religion and Spirituality*. New York: Guilford.

Grotstein, J. (2007). *A Beam of Intense Darkness: Wilfred Bion's Legacy to Psychoanalysis*. Hove, UK: Routledge.

Haidt, J. (2012). *The Righteous Mind*. London: Allen Lane.

Harding, C. (2013). The therapeutic method of Kosawa Heisaku: 'religion' and the 'psy' disciplines. http://ed.ac.uk/schools-departments/history-classic-sarchaeology/ history/research/working-papers (last accessed February 21, 2022).

Henrich, J. (2021). *The Weirdest People in the World: How the West Became Psychologically Peculiar and Particularly Prosperous*. London: Penguin.

Hickel, J. (2021). *Less Is More: How Degrowth Will Save the World*. London: Penguin.

Higginbotham, A. (2012, October 12). Interview with Oliver Sachs. *Daily Telegraph*.

Hitchens, C. (2007). *God Is Not Great: The Case against Religion*. London: Atlantic.

Hobson, A. (2007). Wake up or dream on? Six questions for Turnbull and Solms. *Cortex, 43*: 1113–1115.

Hoffman, D. (2019). *The Case against Reality: How Evolution Hid the Truth from Our Eyes*. London: Penguin.

Holmes, J. (1997). *Attachment, Intimacy, Autonomy*. New York: Jason Aronson.

Holmes, J. (2001). *The Search for the Secure Base*. London: Routledge.

Holmes, J. (2010). *Exploring in Security: Towards an Attachment-informed Psychoanalytic Psychotherapy*. London: Routledge.

Holmes, J. (2020). *The Brain Has a Mind of Its Own*. London: Confer.

Holmes, J., & Slade, A. (2017). *Attachment in Clinical Practice*. London: SAGE.

Holmes, J., & Storr, A. (2024). *The Art of Psychotherapy*. Hove, UK: Routledge.

Hood, B. (2009). *Supersense: From Superstition to Religion—The Brain Science of Belief*. London: Hachette.

Hopkins, G. M. (1953). *Gerard Manley Hopkins*. Penguin Poets. London: Penguin, 1961.

Hopper, E. (Ed.) (2012). *Trauma and Organisations*. London: Karnac.

Hrdy, S. B. (1999). *Mother Nature*. London: Penguin.

Hughes, T. (1968). *A Choice of Emily Dickinson's Verse*. London: Faber.

Humphrey, N. (2023). *Sentience: The Invention of Consciousness*. Cambridge, MA: MIT Press.

Isherwood, C. (1939). *Goodbye to Berlin*. London: Vintage Classics, 1989.

James, W. (1902). *The Varieties of Religious Experience*. London: Folio Society, 2008.

Johns, L., & van Os, J. (2001). The continuity of psychotic experience in the general population. *Clinical Psychology Review, 21*: 1125–1146.

Jordan, J. (2007). *Pascal's Wager: Pragmatic Arguments and Belief in God*. Oxford: Oxford University Press.

Jung, C. G. (1968). *Psychology and Alchemy, Collected Works of C. G. Jung, Volume 12*. Princeton, NJ: Princeton University Press.

Jung, C. G. (1969). *Synchronicity: An Acausal Connecting Principle*. Princeton, NJ: Princeton University Press.

Jung, C. G. (1985). *Modern Man in Search of a Soul*. London: Routledge, 2001.

Keats, J. (2009). *The Complete Poetical Works and Letters of John Keats*. Cambridge Edition. Cambridge: Cambridge University Press.

Kirchhoff, M., & Froese, T. (2017). Where there is life there is mind. *Entropy, 19*(4): 169. https://doi.org/10.3390/e19040169 (last accessed April 14, 2023).

Kushner, H. (2004). *When Bad Things Happen to Good People*. New York: Anchor.

Kuyken, W., Watkins, E., Holden, E., White, K., Taylor, R. S., Byford, S., Evans, A., Radford, S., Teasdale, J. D., & Dalgleish, T. (2010). How does mindfulness-based therapy work? *Behaviour Research and Therapy, 48*(11): 1105–1112.

Lakoff, G., & Johnson, M. (1999). *Philosophy in the Flesh*. New York: Basic Books.

Laland, P. (2017). *Darwin's Unfinished Symphony*. Princeton, NJ: Princeton University Press.

Layard, R., & Clark, D. (2014). *Thrive: The Power of Psychological Therapies*. London: Penguin.

Lear, J. (2011). *A Case for Irony*. Cambridge, MA: Harvard University Press.

Leichsenring, F. (2008). Effectiveness of long-term psychodynamic psychotherapy. *Journal of the American Medical Association, 300*: 1551–1565.

Levy, K., Clarkin, J., Yeomans, F., Scott, L., Wasserman, R., & Kernberg, O. (2006). Mechanisms of change in the treatment of borderline personality disorder treated with transference focused psychotherapy. *Journal of Clinical Psychology, 62*: 481–501.

Linehan, M. M., Comtois, K. A., Murray, A. M., Brown, M. Z., Gallop, R. J., Heard, H. L., Korslund, K. E., Tutek, D. A., Reynolds, S. K., & Lindenboim, N. (2006). Two-year randomized controlled trial and follow-up of dialectical behavior therapy vs therapy by experts for suicidal behaviors and borderline personality disorder. *Archives of General Psychiatry, 63*(7): 757–766.

Main, M., Kaplan, N., & Cassidy, J. (1985). Security in infancy, childhood and adulthood: a move to the level of representation. *Monographs of the Society for Research in Child Development, 50*: 66–104.

Malik, K. (2023, May 12). Vermeer's luminous interiors. *Observer Newspaper.*

Marmot, M. (2016). *The Health Gap.* London: Bloomsbury.

Marx, K., & Engels, F. (1844). *Economic and Philosophical Manuscripts.* M. Milligan (Trans.). Kindle, 2011.

Meares, R. E. (2016). *The Poet's Voice in the Making of Mind.* London: Routledge.

Meins, E. (1997). *Security of Attachment and the Development of Social Cognition.* Hove, UK: Psychology Press.

Mikulincer, M., & Shaver, P. R. (2007). *Attachment in Adulthood: Structure, Dynamics, and Change.* New York: Guilford.

Milner, M. (1987). *The Suppressed Madness of Sane Men.* London: Tavistock.

Mitchell, S. (1993). *Hope and Dread in Psychoanalysis.* New York: Basic Books.

Mueller, P. S., Plevak, D. J., & Rummans, T. A. (2001). Religious involvement, spirituality and health: Implications for clinical practice. *Mayo Clinic Proceedings, 76*(12): 1225–1235. doi/org:10.4065/76.12.1255.

Murray, L., & Andrews, L. (2005). *The Social Baby.* London: CP Publishing.

Music, G. (2014). *The Good Life: Wellbeing and the New Science of Altruism, Selfishness, and Immorality.* London: Routledge.

Neiman, S. (2016). *Why Grow Up?* London: Penguin.

Ogden, T. (2016). *Reclaiming Unlived Life.* London: Routledge.

Olds, S. (2005). *Selected Poems.* London: Cape.

Parfit, D. (1984). *Reasons and Persons.* Oxford: Oxford University Press.

Pargament, K. (2007). *Spiritually Integrated Psychotherapy: Understanding and Addressing the Sacred.* New York: Guilford.

Pargament, K. (Ed.) (2013). *APA Handbook of Religion and Spirituality (Vols. 1 & 2)*. Washington, DC: American Psychological Association.

Pearson, J., Cohn, D., Cowan, C., & Cohn, D. (1994). Earned- and continuous-security in adult attachment: Relation to depressive symptomatology and parenting style. *Development and Psychopathology, 6*: 359–373.

Rawls, J. (2001). *Justice as Fairness: A Restatement*. Cambridge, MA: Belknap Press.

Reibstein, J. (2023). *Good Relations*. London: Bloomsbury.

Resnick, J. (2023). *Meaning-Fullness: Developmental Psychotherapy and the Pursuit of Mental Health*. London: Karnac.

Rovelli, C. (2022). *Helgoland: The Strange and Beautiful Story of Quantum Physics*. London: Penguin.

Rustin, M. (2019). *Researching the Unconscious*. London: Routledge.

Rycroft, C. (1996). *The Innocence of Dreams*. London: Karnac.

Safran, J. (Ed.) (2003). *Psychoanalysis and Buddhism: An Unfolding Dialogue*. Boston, MA: Wisdom.

Sahdra, B. K., & Shaver, P. R. (2013). Comparing attachment theory and Buddhist psychology. *International Journal for the Psychology of Religion, 23*: 282–293.

Schore, A. (2001). Effects of a secure attachment relationship on right brain development. *Infant Mental Health Journal, 22*: 7–66.

Schrödinger, E. (1944). *What Is Life?* Cambridge: Cambridge University Press, 2012.

Seth, A. (2022). *Being You: A New Science of Consciousness*. London: Penguin.

Shakespeare, W. (1611). *The Tempest*. Act I, scene 2, line 565. London: Nonesuch, 1968.

Shedler, J. (2010). The efficacy of psychodynamic psychotherapy. *American Psychologist, 65*: 98–110.

Slade, A., & Holmes, J. (Eds.) (2014). Introduction. *Attachment Theory*. London: SAGE.

Solms, M. (2021). *The Hidden Spring: Journey to the Source of Consciousness*. London: Profile.

Sorenson, R. (2004). *Minding Spirituality*. Hillsdale, NJ: Analytic Press.

Spufford, F. (2013). *Unapologetic: Why, Despite Everything, Christianity Can Still Make Surprising Emotional Sense*. London: Bloomsbury.

Stallings, A. (2023). Frieze frame. *Hudson Review*, Spring.

Stern, D. (1985). *The Interpersonal World of the Infant*. New York: Basic Books.

Stern, D. (2010). *Partners in Thought: Working with Unformulated Experience, Dissociation, and Enactment.* London: Routledge.

Stuart-Smith, S. (2020). *The Well Gardened Mind: Rediscovering Nature in the Modern World.* London: Collins.

Symington, N. (1998). *Emotion and Spirit: Questioning the Claims of Psycho-analysis and Religion.* London: Tavistock.

Taylor, C. (2007). *A Secular Age.* Cambridge, MA: Belknap Press.

Thich Nhat Hanh (2011). *Your True Home.* New York: Shambhala.

Thomas, D. (1957). The force that through the green fuse drives the flower. In: *Collected Poems.* London: Faber.

Tolle, E. (1999). *The Power of Now.* London: Hodder.

Tolstoy, L. (1869). *War and Peace.* R. Edmonds (Trans.). London: Penguin, 1978.

Tronick, E., & Gold, C. M. (2020). *The Power of Discord: Why the Ups and Downs of Relationships Are the Secret to Building Intimacy, Resilience, and Trust.* Abingdon, UK: Scribe.

Vaillant, G. E. (1993). *The Wisdom of the Ego: Sources of Resilience in Adult Life.* Cambridge, MA: Harvard University Press.

Vaillant, G. E. (2008). *Spiritual Evolution: How We Are Wired for Faith, Hope and Love.* New York: Broadway.

Vaillant, G. E. (2009). *Spiritual Evolution: A Scientific Defense of Faith.* New York: Random House.

Van Deurzen, E., & Kenward, R. (2005). *Dictionary of Existential Psychother-apy and Counselling.* London: SAGE.

Van IJzendoorn, M. H., & Bakermans-Kranenburg, M. J. (2012). A sniff of trust: Meta-analysis of the effects of intranasal oxytocin administration on face recognition, trust to in-group and trust to out-group. *Psychoendocri-nology, 37*: 438–443.

Wampold, B. (2015). How important are common factors in psychotherapy? *World Psychiatry, 14*: 270–277.

Whitaker, P. (2021, December 8). Knowing patients well can be life-saving. *New Statesman.*

Wilkinson, R., & Pickett, K. (2009). *The Spirit Level: Why More Equal Societies Almost Always Do Better.* London: Allen Lane.

Williams, R. (2012). *Faith in the Public Square.* London: Bloomsbury

Wilson, D. S. (2019). *This View of Life: Completing the Darwinian Revolution.* New York: Pantheon.

Winnicott, D. W. (1962). *The Maturational Processes and the Facilitating Environment*. London: Hogarth.

Winnicott, D. W. (1992). *Psycho-Analytic Explorations*. Cambridge, MA: Harvard University Press.

Wright, K. (2006). Preverbal experience and intuition of the sacred. In: D. Black (Ed.), *Religion and Psychoanalysis in the 21st Century*. London: Routledge.

Yalom, I. (1980). *Existential Psychotherapy*. New York: Basic Books.

Yeats, W. B. (1899). 'Aedh wishes for the cloths of heaven'. In: *Wordsworth Poetry Library: Collected Poems of W. B. Yeats*. London: Wordsworth, 2008.

Index